How to Succeed in Life

Published by :
Lotus Press Publishers & Distributors

How to Succeed in Life

Moses Michael

Lotus PRESS

4735/22, Prakash Deep Building
Ansari Road, Darya Ganj,
New Delhi - 110002

Lotus Press : Publishers & Distributors
Unit No. 220, 2nd Floor, 4735/22, Prakash Deep Building,
Ansari Road, Darya Ganj, New Delhi- 110002
Ph.: 23280047, 98118-38000
• E-mail : lotuspress1984@gmail.com
www.lotuspress.co.in

How to Succeed in Life

ISBN: 978-81-8382-336-4

Printed & Published by : **Lotus Press Publisher & Distributors,** New Delhi-02

PREFACE

Although intention, dedication, determination, concentration, perseverance, etc., are key words to Success, different areas of work demand, slightly differently these factors for somebody who wants to be successful. The foremost quality of a businessman is to be quite an enterprising one. A professional should be more ambitious than anything else. A scholar should have a studious character, in him to make himself a success. A politician needs to remain diplomatic and friendly in his dealings with people. A wise individual always prefers to a have a look at the demands of a particular area.

This book is the outcome of long contemplation and extensive study in this area of enormous interest. It deals with almost all the aspects of human activities and all needs and demands of these spheres.

—Author

CONTENTS

Preface v

1. Success in Life **9**

Levels of Success
Capacity and Character
Social Environment
Human Initiative
Character of Life
Hidden Patterns
Human Choice
Unfailing Success
Responsibility and Growth
Response to Opportunities
Involution and Evolution
Optimal Accomplishment
Inner Techniques

2. Skills for Success **44**

Overview of the Curriculum
The Assertiveness
Social Skills

3. Dynamism and Enthusiasm **56**

Forging Self-confidence
Removing Negative Thoughts
How to Change Your Life?
Positive Attitude
Choosing Success
Incredible Power of Focus

Success through Goal-Setting
Great Success Preceded by Great Failure
Achieving Dreams
Managing Time
Project Management
Transforming Bad Habits
Goal Orientation
Result Orientation
Action Orientation
People Orientation
Health Orientation
Honesty and Integrity
Self-discipline
Formula for Failure and Success
Real Action
Preparing for Future

4. Stress Management **138**
Health
Nutrition
Controlling Stress
Negation of Destructive Behaviour
Appropriate Medical Advice
Using Sick Time Benefits

5. Crisis Management **160**
Anger Management
Recognising Anger
Coping Skills-Relaxation
Coping Skills-Self-talk
Conflict Resolution
Steps to Resolve
Getting along with Co-workers
Leisure Skills
Decision Making
Problem-Solving Procedures

1

SUCCESS IN LIFE

In this topic we endeavour to uncover the keys to great accomplishment in life. Often people believe that to be successful in life requires some luck and a few skills, yet our research shows that it is a much richer set of factors that come into play that determine whether or not one accomplishes or fails in any endeavour. *First* we'll discuss the different levels that a person can accomplish at—*i.e.*, survival, growth, development and evolution.

Then we'll examine the capacities and character that an individual has to have in order to accomplish. These include his skills, attitudes, values and other factors. We'll also consider how an individual relates to the social institutions in which he tries to accomplish. Does he conform or think "beyond the box?" Then we'll discuss how the capacities and character of the social institutions he interacts with to accomplish affect the final outcome. We'll then uncover some of the hidden secrets and patterns of life that are at play as an individual tries to accomplish in life.

LEVELS OF SUCCESS

Before we discuss the factors that come into play that account for great accomplishments in life, let's discuss different levels of accomplishment that an individual can accomplish at. From our experience we have observed that there are four fundamental levels at which an individual can accomplish-*survival, growth, development and evolution.*

Survival: Living at the survival level one has a conscious or unconscious desire to *remain at the current level* of achievement in life. There is no attempt to rise above one's current achievement, nor is there an effort to raise one's own personal capacities. There is neither a quantitative expansion at one's current level of life, let alone a qualitative movement to a potential higher-level.

A real world example of accomplishment at the level of survival is an instructor who has achieved a degree of success that keeps him comfortable, has a defined set of skills and has no desire or makes no effort, to acquire more work or perhaps even update his skills to be current to the present needs of his students.

Growth: Growth, on the other hand, is an *expansion of one's current level of* achievement. *For example,* improving on a skill, expanding knowledge in a field or another field at the same level and earning more through greater effort are each expressions of growth. You are accomplishing more, but it is more at the *same* level. It is a *horizontal* expansion at the same level of capacity and achievement; *i.e.,* an *expansion of one's current level of achievement.*

To accomplishment at the level of growth the instructor would learn the latest versions of the current programmes he is teaching and seek out work with other companies to teach the same things he has been teaching in the past. He would be aspiring for more of the same work.

Development: Development, on the other hand, is an *expansion to a higher-level* of achievement. One may acquire a new or *higher-level skill,* accept and implement a *higher* personal value, change a negative personal attitude into a positive attitude, acquire a higher order of knowledge, develops a new faith in life or in general respond from a higher centre than one's current level of development and consciousness. These are all expressions of personal development. In all these instances you are accomplishing at a *higher-level*, not merely more at the same level. Thus, we say that it is a *vertical* expansion to a new level of capacity and achievement.

In our real world example at the level of development our instructor could have an aspiration to teach whole new subjects that are outside of his normal curricula, make contact with new types of clients, so he can teach these courses, write a book on the topic of this new area, change a few personal attitudes in his life (such as attitudes towards his superiors) or decide to more fully implement in his work a value that he already cherishes, such as the value that students should come away with real knowledge in his classroom, rather than mere satisfaction of the experience.

Evolution: *Evolution is an elevation of one's being to a whole new higher plane of consciousness and status of being. For example,* an emotional individual could shift from the state where his desires and attachments pre-dominate to becoming a person of more refined or higher emotions; or move from being a predominantly emotional person to becoming a more mental and thoughtful person whose life shifts from one of emotional intensity to thoughtfulness. Perhaps the individual rises to acquiring spiritual capacities, such as the ability to experience knowledge as illuminations of light or intuition or to find his personal evolving soul.

In these instances you are accomplishing from a *higher plane of consciousness* than you were from before. It is a *vertical leap* to a new plane of capacity and achievement; an elevation of one's being to a *whole new higher plane of consciousness.*

In our real world example of accomplishment at the level of evolution our instructor could change from being a person who competently performs his courses in an orderly and efficient manner to an individual who is passionate about teaching and emotionally involved with his students.

He may also develop whole new theories of instruction based on his new level of consciousness, rather than merely being a teacher of existing ideas. His overall attitudes toward his work has completely changed to the positive. He might move from emotional interaction with students to a true knowledge; even utilising spiritual methods as a foundation for his work.

Transformation: At the frontiers of the development of the being is the transformation of the individual to a whole other functioning in life. One can embody a permanent inner change that connects one to the inner soul being one can enable a spiritual transformation into the spiritual planes of life above mind; and one can make the ultimate supramental transformation into a whole new type of being, beyond even the human functioning we now witness. As we embody these three transformational frontiers, we open to the infinite potentials of life, where we can thus accomplish infinitely in life.

Things to Think About: Based on this discussion consider which level of accomplishment you are currently at—survival, growth, development, evolution or transformation (most people are at the first level). Then consider how you could move to the next highest type (*e.g.*, survival to growth, growth to development, development to evolution).

Think of some other people who have moved among the levels. Do you know of a person who abruptly changed course, say from the level of growth (more of the same) to that of development (to a whole new qualitative level of accomplishment). If so, discover the history and aspects of that person's life that enabled that leap to take place. Consider how you would do something similar in your life. Do you also know of someone who has made a radical change of character, making what one would call an evolutionary leap?

CAPACITY AND CHARACTER

Accomplishment is, to a large extent, determined by the individual's *capacities*, which in total are demonstrated in life as the person's *character*. Our individual capacities in life are made up a combination of a number of factors including our skills and *knowledge* in the world, our *attitudes* about ourselves, others and things, our miscellaneous *attributes* (such as our level of clarity of goals, organisation, psychological strength, energy, ambition, perseverance and general health, amongst others); our *endowments* (such as the role our parents played in motivating us and what they provided us and the influence of the society we live in) and our personal values (such as a belief in being practical or being results-oriented).

Together these skills, knowledge, attitudes, attributes and values constitute our capacities to function in the world. The degree to which we have them determines our abilities to accomplish in life. Any effort to improve ourselves in any of these areas will surely go a long way to improving our ability to accomplish in life.

Results, accomplishment, success in life are determined by the right intensities of these aspects of our being.

Below is a list of sample factors that determine our capacities and character in life. The factors are grouped into five categories–our attitudes, attributes, skills, endowments and values. Review this list and determine where your strengths and weaknesses lie. Pick out a few factors within each of the categories that you think you might be lacking in and think about how you can uplift yourself by making an improvement in those areas.

Then come up with a real plan to improve yourself in that area. Finally, carry out the plan with great determination. You are sure to see great improvements in your life, including greater accomplishment, achievement, success and happiness.

Example: Let's then turn to the instructor and note his positive and negative capacities to accomplish. On examination we determine that he is intelligent, creative, resourceful, diligent, faithful, cheerful, has goodwill, is sincere and frank and has aspirations for improvement. These tendencies will help in his initiatives for accomplishment. On the other hand, he can be close-minded, aloof, hunger for attention, be unresponsive to opportunities that appear and be lacking in physical energy.

In summary, the cumulative capacity, energy and force of being, *i.e.,* character, largely determines one's ability to accomplish in life. One can at any time make the effort to improve in any of these areas, especially where one is lacking, which will surely dramatically increase one's abilities to achieve and succeed in life.

Things to Think About: Pick one or two items in each category where you think you are lacking. Then make the sincere, concerted and unflagging effort to improve yourself in that area; in any aspect of your work, career or other parts of your life.

So far we have said that an individual can accomplish at the level of survival, growth, development and evolution. In addition, the individual's ultimate potential for accomplishment seems to be determined by his physical, vital, emotional and mental energies and capacities, i.e. his character. There is of course, the external world in which he will carry out acts in an attempt to accomplish.

How he perceives that world may go a long way to establishing the scope at which he can accomplish. Before we examine the nature of the social institutions that he will interact with and how they will effect his ability to accomplish, we should discuss an individual's potential dispositions toward the outside world. Does he feel alienated from the world, does he feel part of world and obliged to its modes of thinking or does he have an exceptional talent that transcends normal thinking, mores and values?

Social Character: One person may fit in well within the social conventions of the time; another may not. If the person who fits in well with the social conventions has the skills, knowledge, energy, organisation, attitudes, values and aspirations in life, he can accomplish fully within the constraints of the social environment in which he partakes. We can say that this individual has a developed social character. He is one with the social aspirations, goals, rules, functionings, etc., of the social institution he partakes in (whether he makes full use of this environment is a separate issue).

Assuming the society around him allows for it, a person with social character can establish his own business, raise a family and accomplish a substantial work in the society. On the other hand, if an individual with social character also has a noble or weighty character, he may even be able to accomplish to the level of becoming a philanthropist or a CEO.

Individual Character: On the other hand, the individual who has developed *individual* character has the potential to accomplish at a far greater level. This person thinks for himself (*i.e.* "beyond the box"), which in turn opens far greater vistas and a greater scope for accomplishment, achievement and success. That's not to say that he rejects the society he is a part of.

On the contrary, he has fully absorbed and assimilated the present social environment and its conventions and ideas. The difference is that he has taken these a step further by personalising, individualising them with his own values, attitudes and energies.

An example of this would be Steve Jobs when he first developed Apple. There his desire to make a computer that people were not afraid of or intimidated by to use, was something that went beyond conventional wisdom.

Other examples are Fred Smith, founder of Federal Express and Jeff Bezos, founder of Amazon. The person with individual character rises to the level of his personal ideals and values; values such as being flexible, open-minded and resourceful; demonstrating character that might not normally be associated with society or the social institutions in which he partakes.

Things to Think About: How can you express your own individuality more and think and act "outside of the box."

What are your deepest personal values and how can you express them so that you can accomplish at unprecedented levels in your life.

SOCIAL ENVIRONMENT

Beyond the individual's aspiration, capacities and character there are the actual social forces at play that lie beyond the individual's capacities or perceptions of the social environment. These include:

(*a*) the real world situations, circumstances and atmosphere that the individual finds himself in; including the social institutions he is interacting with;

(*b*) the social level he is at vs. the social level of the people he is interacting with at the social institution;

(*c*) the character of the social institution itself, including its tendencies, movement and growth path; and

(*d*) the movements and tendencies of the society in general in which he and the social institutions he partakes in are part of. All of these come into play as he takes his own capacities and social perceptions into this field of life. Together they determine the outcome of his ability to accomplish in life.

Let's put aside factor a and b for now and focus on factor c for a moment; the character of the social institution itself, including its tendencies, movement and growth path. Consider the impact of the character of a social institution, such as the employer that the individual works for, on the individual. If an individual works for a company where the collective will of the company is very strong, but where the role and the opinions of individuals are stifled, he could be severely limited in his ability to accomplish within that company to the degree he expresses his individuality. Likewise, if the company puts its resources (knowledge, power, privilege and wealth) only in the hands of an elite few and if he is not in the elite, he will again be limited in his ability to accomplish. The same is true if he is part of a forgotten, ignored or weaker part of the company, his possibilities may be limited.

Thus, we can see that the character of the social institution has a dramatic effect on his ability to accomplish. The social institution can help or harm the individual through its level of organisation, knowledge and skills of its people, attitudes, perceptions, values, etc.; factors that are in fact similar to the factors that determine an individual's capacities and character.

Furthermore, we can also witness the fact that there is a hierarchy of affects. The social institution itself is affected by the mores, attitudes, values, rules, procedures and possibilities of the community and society in which it resides.

Accomplishment is influenced then by the individual's aspirations and capacities, as well as the hierarchy of capacities and character of the institutions and super institutions (*i.e.*, the community or greater society itself) in which he tries to accomplish.

Things to Think About: Are you availing yourself of the opportunities your social institutions (*e.g.*, employer, community, nation, etc.) are currently presenting to you? Are the social institutions you partake in supportive of your initiatives for accomplishment or they a hindrance? What are the limitations of the social institution? What action should you take as a result?

Related Info: If you would like to find out how a company can best support the growth and development of its employees and make that its highest business value, If you would like to find out how society can best support the growth and development of people.

HUMAN INITIATIVE

When we try to accomplish something in life through our initiative it may or may not succeed. Here, are some of the subtle workings that affect the success of failure of any initiative.

- When the social atmosphere is positive with regard to an initiative, the atmosphere fosters success for the individual. When the atmosphere is negative, the individual's initiative will fail, unless he is able to overcome the resistance of the atmosphere.

  Example: In a community there is a very positive feeling towards improving the education. An individual begins an initiative to improve the quality of the courseware. On the surface she initially fails; yet the initiative is taken up by another person and succeeds with it. That is because there is a positive atmosphere in the community as it relates to education. (If there were a negative atmosphere toward education, the initiative would have failed all around).

  Example: As indicated in the book The Three Musketeers. "Whatever the liberality of the day, the story takes place in an age when the belief in good is quite pervasive and religious issues dominate society. In fact, if one law seems to express throughout the story, it is the resistance to illicit love at higher levels of society. Buckingham's advances to Anne lead to his death. Constance's two attempts to unite with D'Artagnan are frustrated, the first by her arrest, the second by her death. Even Milady's passion for de Wardes is frustrated by D'Artagnan. Aramis returns to religion, not to his aristocratic lover. Only Porthos who seeks money, not love and stoops to the level of the proprietress succeeds and that too by marriage. There is no instance of illicit love prospering in the story" (MSS).

- Initiatives fail when taken outside one's field of influence, authority or control.

  Example: A man tries to create a higher sense of moral authority in the community. The community has actually transcended his morality with an openness to new ideas that the individual can not fathom. His initiative to bring about moral authority fails.

- Initiatives from lower levels of life do not have power for accomplishment at higher-levels of life.

  Example: A consultant was asked by his superiors to investigate the development of tool to allow for on-line student training evaluations. He worked on it for months without ever clarifying with his superior the pay he would receive as well as the timeframe on the project. He was too intimidated to make these clarifications. Ultimately the project failed completely and the consultant wasted months of his time.

  Example: X tries to influence Y's opinion about Z. X's efforts to influence Y's opinion of Z fail because X is stationed at a lower level of the social hierarchy than Y. It is the higher station that sets the standards for what is or is not acceptable or fashionable.

- On the other hand, initiatives by those in a higher plane of life (*i.e.,* with greater wealth, status or power) toward those in a lower plane tend to be readily and richly fulfilled, provided the lower is a willing recipient and does not raise obstacles or resistance to receiving. This principle acts in the same manner as water flowing downhill.

  Example: A manager of a training company wanted to have her instructors do training on a new software programme. Many happily agreed to it and received basic knowledge on the programme from the training company. After a number of months, the training by the instructors went very well for the training company's clients and even led to additional profitable training on related new products.

- Initiatives may receive unexpected support from life when they are aligned with new movements in life that are gaining momentum. On the other hand, initiatives may meet with unexpected resistance when they are aligned with movements that are passing out of existence.

  Example: X's efforts to marry her daughter Y to Z for social purposes meet with resistance and ultimately fail. X seeks to capitalise on the mutual pledge of her sister and herself that their children should marry, a practise whose value is passing out of existence. The light in Y's eyes that X feels is enough to overcome the best-laid plans of the older generation to perpetuate itself in the old style.

  Example: A man tries to create a higher sense of moral authority in the community. The community has actually transcended his morality with an openness to new ideas that the individual can not fathom. His initiative to bring about moral authority fails.

- Initiatives succeed when taken with sufficient energy and capacity to reverse previous actions that failed as the result of an inappropriate attitude or behaviour.

  Example: A man tries to break up the marriage of his child and succeeds for a time. After a change of heart, he decides that his decision was very foolish and he tries to patch things up. The success of his initiative to change will only occur if he has sufficient vigour to do so and if he gains the agreement of the parties who were initially involved.

These are some of the major forces at play that affect the success or failure of any initiative that a person takes in life. There are movements of life that are normally hidden from us, but are at play in the field of life.

CHARACTER OF LIFE

As we examine the forces at play that affect our ability to accomplish, we are led to think about the fundamental basis by which acts and events in life take place. Such an analysis will give us more insight into the ability to accomplish in life.

Acts: The individual meets life through acts. Individual acts are the fundamental unit of life and action. They are the building blocks of activity and motion, *i.e.,* life. The ways these acts are acted out have an ultimate effect on the ability of the individual to accomplish in life. Into every act the individual takes his level of aspiration, capacities and character, social perception and meets the social forces around him. The result and accomplishment is determined by the mix of these forces.

A series of acts make up the interaction, events, situations and circumstances of life. We can also perhaps say that the play of life is the story of how the acts unfold, of whether or not there was accomplishment. *For example,* in his plays Shakespeare portrays a series of acts that occur in a timeline that make up a play. Through a series of acts he clearly portrays the individual and social forces and the outcomes that result, either good or bad (*i.e.,* tragedies).

Analysing the Causes of Accomplishment and Failure: We can observe a person's initiative to accomplish and see if it plays out successfully or unsuccessfully as he acts it out in the game of life. For any initiative to accomplish we can come to understand how an individual's capacities and character play out against the social forces he confronts. If his capacities and character are optimal and the character and forces of society, including the social institutions in which the act is carried out are optimal, he cannot help but succeed. The reverse is of course also true.

We can learn much about our ability to accomplish in literature and in the other arts. Shakespeare for one is a gold mine for viewing a variety of situations and circumstances in which humans try to accomplish. Looking at it from the perspective of the capacities and character of the individual we witness plethora of examples. *For example,* we can observe how Hamlet's indecisiveness in the presence of great evil done leads to his own downfall. We see how Romeo and Juliet are overwhelmed by their passions and emotions. We see how King Lear goes mad because he is so attached to a daughter who refuses his overture of inheritance.

In each case we see the aspiration and strengths and weaknesses of individual character played out against a social background as they try to accomplish that which is dear to them. In essence, they fail; hence they are tragic figures. We can also witness the social context in which human acts occur. *For Example* Romeo and Juliet's death occur as their acts of intensity and passion are played out against a social context of lurking conflict between the Montagues and Capulets. This further intensifies their situation, leading to their tragedy, as well as society's tragedy and eventual reconciliation.

In the real play of life we can observe the same forces that lead to accomplishment or failure (or even tragedy). If we were to observe our lives as a detached observer such as a Shakespeare (or a God!), it would be possible to examine our own situations or the situations of others and see what were the individual and social forces that led to accomplishment or failure. In fact, one could think about any great accomplishment or failure in our lives and examine the conditions that existed that could foster positive or negative results. We would need to examine our aspirations, our capacities and character, our social and individual character and the character of the social environment, including the direct social character of the institutions we interacted with. Certainly such a self-examination would reveal the major forces at work that led to accomplishment or failure.

HIDDEN PATTERNS

Yet, as we draw even closer to the events, we begin to unravel a whole other, deeper layer that seems to go beyond our current abilities to analyse the situation. It's as if we were examining molecules to understand the workings of the body, only to come across the much smaller atoms that make up the molecules. Not only that the atoms were working in mysterious unfathomable ways that defy cause and effect and our natural, rational abilities to understand things.

Take for instance the situation where one individual appears in a scene in a Shakespeare play and then another appears in that scene at the same time. Our normal reaction is to just watch the scene unfold and not make anything of the fact that they both appeared on the scene at the same time. There is obvious no relationship between the two occurrences; they simply seem to be happing at the same time, that's all. At most we might think that it is mere coincidence and nothing more. However, on closer examination we start to uncover patterns that suggest that incidences like this are not random, but are part of a pattern that is beyond our normal perceptions. These are the hidden, yet astounding patterns of life that defy our awareness, yet may prove to be the ultimate determinant of accomplishment in life.

> *"The pattern of interaction between character, action and the results of action reveals the importance of a crucial in determinant which is variously called providence, chance, fate, etc. What appears as chance at the level of physical action is an expression of another*

dimension of causality in the plane of life. Shakespeare possessed an intuitive insight into this realm and into the role of individual character and social consciousness as points of expression of the wider character of life."

These types of occurrences are going on in Shakespeare's plays and they are going on in our daily lives, yet we are oblivious of them, let alone not conscious of any pattern in their occurrences. Yet our research indicates that these occurrences do in fact have patterns behind them and that the patterns indicate a subtle and complex working of life that reflect on the actions, perceptions, attitudes, energies, environment of the individuals and social environment that are involved.

Let's talk about one phenomenon we have uncovered, called "life response." A life response is an instantaneous positive response/occurrence in life to an act that an individual takes. Here's an example:

An instructor had not been contacted for new work for weeks and was in desperate straits. He decided to apply the idea of cleanliness. His apartment was normally quite clean, but he wanted to take cleanliness a step further. He decided to clean his refrigerator, something he was reluctant to do. At the exact moment he finished putting things back into the refrigerator after cleaning, he heard a message on his answering machine from the his training company offering him new work. The response from life was instantaneous!

Though this is an example of how life responds to an initiative of improving the cleanliness or orderliness of something one can also elicit a life response in a number of ways–by inwardly overcoming a negative attitude, by overcoming one's hesitation to do something important, by acknowledging a defect or making an effort to understand a weakness and in many other ways. In each case life seems to trigger something positive for us and often very fast. This process of life defies all logic, yet it is an aspect of life that occurs all of the time. If we learn to channelise its power we can accomplish anything in life.

We have seen many other hidden patterns of life that reflect on whether we accomplish in life. *For example*, we have often seen how certain acts seem to repeat at certain intervals, revealing a hidden meaning that is reflecting on whether accomplishment is occurring. Or we have seen signs of how people are related in a situation just from how they appear simultaneously in a situation. To the surface mind, there is absolutely no meaning to this, but on closer examination they give us clues of a pattern of the workings of life which when understood can help us determine in which situation accomplishment will occur and when it won't.

By understanding these hidden working of life, one can begin to gain a new level of mastery over life. By learning to trigger life responses in one's life, one can dramatically accelerate accomplishment; and by reading the hidden signs of life one gains an insight and knowledge about life that enables one to take right action in situations, which can only help in one's endeavour to accomplish in life. To review explanations of and examples of these hidden patterns of life which can help you accomplish greater in life.

Follow-up Reading: The hidden workings of life have been suggested in many of the myths, religions and arts of various cultures, including the world's literature. For a discussion of how these hidden planes of life reveal themselves in literature and how we can see the same patterns in our real lives.

HUMAN CHOICE

Though these many forces come into play in life there is a fundamental force that directs our lives. It is our own will and desires in life that to a great extent determine the outcomes in life. If a man wants financial security in his life, then his action, whether he is conscious of it or not, will lead him to become more secure in life. Therefore, we can say that the ultimate determinent factor in our lives is human choice, what we really desire and will in the first place. Whatever we desire, be it financial security, love, high position, fame, creative outlet, high achievement, etc. or any combination of these will ultimately effect the outcome of achievement and happiness in life.

This is not to say that our capacities and character, the social atmosphere and conditions and the other hidden patterns of life that we have outlined above won't come into play. It is just to point out that the starting point for most outcomes in our lives is our inner wants and desires, which we are given the freedom to seek out in our lives. We may not get to our deepest desires in the manner expected, but ultimately we are moving in that direction.

A man wondered why no matter how hard he tried that he never really became prosperous. He then thought back on his life to his early 20's and remembered how idealistic he was; how he really wanted to write about the new changes in the world and otherwise educate others to new developments and possibilities. He later became an instructor who taught others and he edited a web site where he explained new age ideas for personal and social growth. (Up to that time he never became prosperous because gaining wealth was never critical to his life. He could, of course, change course and could make prosperity a central driving force in his life if he truly wished to do so. It's his choice).

Accomplishment and the Sanction of One's Emotions: Here is another way of putting it. An individual may think about ways to improve himself, but that is not enough to accomplish a thing in life. He can even try (*i.e.,*) to accomplish something at a greater level, but that might not bring in the desired results. When the mind decides to accomplish something it needs the sanction of the vital, the emotions. When there is a desire, a deep emotion to accomplish a thing, it gains force and will of purpose. Thought to accomplish a thing without the emotional desire and need, will ultimately leave things as they are. When the sanction of the emotions is obtained, accomplishment of the thing gathers force and attracts positive circumstance from life.

For example, an individual might want to earn more money in his life. However, at an emotional level this individual might feel secure and self-satisfied in his current state (he may or not be conscious that he feels this way!). Perhaps he seeks freedom more than material gain as money. He will not accomplish what his mind thinks is necessary. Money will not come to such an individual, even if he thinks he needs more money. On the other hand a deep-felt want, hunger, ambition for money will unleash positive responses from life and money will be attracted to such an individual. Furthermore, if he takes a physical action, *i.e.,* he acts on this emotion, he completes the process that will attract money to him in his life he has gathered the full force to accomplish.

UNFAILING SUCCESS

Is it possible to insure that any activity we undertake in our lives ends in a perfect and unending success? We believe it can, so long as you understand the key factors that can create this condition. Regardless of your field of work, level at which you do your work or the circumstances involved in your work, our research has shown that there are three essential conditions that need to be met for unfailing success to occur in any activity, goal or pursuit.

1. *Total Commitment:* Your decision, determination and desire to accomplish the activity, goal or pursuit should be total and complete, to the point that it releases the full energies of your personality and generates an overflowing enthusiasm to convert that determination into action.

Energy is the basis for all accomplishment. Human energy is released when your mind, emotions and vital personality fully endorse and eagerly pursue the same goal. Where there is inner conflict or hesitation or where you act out of an understanding or accepted ideal that the emotions do not fully endorse, the release of energy will be limited and therefore the results will be limited too. Total commitment is based on total knowledge and understanding of the requirements of the act and the role of both helpful and opposing forces.

2. *Positive Opinions and Attitudes:* All your thoughts, opinions, attitudes and motives concerning the activity should be fully positive. By "positive" we mean free of all negative elements, such as falsehood, dishonesty, exaggeration, selfishness, jealousy, anger, irritation, impatience, greed, fear, laziness, etc.

   We are not saying that you must be transformed into a saint or a yogi or even an ideal human being, but with respect to the specific activity, you should elevate your thoughts, feelings and attitudes to the highest level of which you are capable. You may be acting for your own personal benefit, which we may term selfish, but you are always capable of considering and carrying out that action in such a way that it does not harm and may also fully benefit other people associated with the act, such as the person with whom you are negotiating a sale or purchase.

   To be positive means that your energies are fully released and flow out in constructive expressions at the level of thought, words, feelings and acts, rather than getting caught up in inner or external conflicts and confrontations which waste the energy unproductively. In essence, this means to act out of the highest personal values of which you are capable with respect to every aspect of this activity.

3. *Perfect Execution:* Make an exhaustive and complete physical effort. Achievement in any field requires an enormous investment of energy and painstaking physical execution. Unfailing success requires that the energy be full and the execution perfect. You can not achieve unfailing success if your actions fall short in terms of the skill or effort or perseverance required for achievement in this field. Make an exhaustive and complete physical effort. Achievement in any field requires an enormous investment of energy and painstaking physical execution. Unfailing success requires that the energy be full and the execution perfect.

KNOWLEDGE, WILL, ENERGY AND ACCOMPLISHMENT

The inner mental, vital and emotional energy one has to accomplish is an expression of one's will. Will itself is a power that comes from knowledge. So the extent of the energy that one releases is determined by the breadth of one's knowledge; the more knowledge, the more energy. *For example,* the more we are aware of the possibilities in life, the more out will is engaged, which releases out energy to accomplish aspects of that knowledge.

What then maximises our knowledge? Education is one. Generally those who are educated accomplish more than those who are not. One can also avail of the social resources there in the collective, which gives a greater capacity than what education gives. The true achiever is energised to accomplish through the knowledge of his own personal resources; *i.e.,* knowledge his own personal and true self.

RESPONSIBILITY AND GROWTH

Throughout our lives we are confronted with external pressures that bear greatly on us. It is how we react to these pressures that determine to a large extent how we accomplish in life. Those who take responsibility, see their own weakness as it relates to the problem, grow and accomplish.

Those who blame others or ignore the pressures stagnate and achieve less. *For example,* in the book Pride and Prejudice the main hero of the book Darcy is confronted by great pressures in life, many of which he created himself in the first place. Fortunately he responds positively to the pressures by *taking personal responsibility for his actions by acknowledging his character flaws and misdeeds.* This acknowledgment and acceptance causes him to grow as an individual, which sets the stage for life to respond positively in kind.

Let's examine how Darcy is confronted with two possible ways to respond and then see how he took responsibility, which created a great positive response from life:

> *Darcy's proposal to Eliza and his insistence on an explanation for her refusal releases a torrent of her resentment and animosity against him.... He has the option of fully justifying his behaviour... and discarding ... accusations as prejudiced or ill informed, in which case he learns nothing about himself and remains where and what he was. Alternatively, he can ignore and excuse her misconceptions and recognise the underlying truth in her accusation that he is ungentlemanly, arrogant and undesirable, which is what he chooses to do. The self-knowledge resulting from that choice of objective self-scrutiny generates an intense pressure on him to modify his behaviour and character to live up in practise to the principles of generosity and goodness that he had all along believed himself to possess.*
>
> *Darcy makes a conscious decision and willed effort to give up his proud and arrogant sense of superiority, his aloof behaviour, his unwillingness to interact with those of lower social status. He not only tries to*

> *eliminate the offensive behaviours of the past. He takes a conscious decision to reverse these characteristics and act in a diametrically opposite direction.*

Having taken this inner and outer initiative to improve himself... life brings two magnificent responses.

On the other hand, another individual confronted by the same great pressures of life fails to take responsibility, blames others and doesn't grow or accomplish in life as a result. Again using a character Mrs. Bennet, mother of the daughters who seek marriage in Pride and Prejudice:

> *She misses no opportunity to fault Wickham, her family and Colonel Forester for her misfortune, but never for an instant reflects on her own most central contribution or expresses a moments shame or regret for her conduct. Mrs. Bennet refuses to become conscious of herself, refuses to exercise her will, refuses any effort to change. She gathers all the energy generated in her by the crisis and throws it out as anger, bitter accusation, sullen disappointment, nervous discomfort and physical complaint.*

When life bears down on us and exerts pressures we can respond positively or negatively. Those who respond positively, who take responsibility rather than blame others or be in different, grow as individuals and set the stage for great positive responses from life and great achievement and happiness.

RESPONSE TO OPPORTUNITIES

How we respond to the opportunities that life presents us is an important key to accomplishing in life. When presented with an opportunity one person may embrace it while another may ignore it or feel indifferent to it. Those who embrace it are put on the fast track to success while those who ignore it stay where they are on regress. Most individuals are somewhere in between, reacting to opportunity in a sluggish manner over a prolonged period of time.

If we become more conscious in our lives, if we are open and our attitudes, opinions and habits don't get in the way, we will be eager to embrace new opportunities when they come our way; opportunities that can make the difference between limited success and great achievement in life.

As we said because we are not conscious enough to perceive and respond positively to opportunities that come our way, often people respond to opportunities in a sluggish manner. That prolonged and troubled occurs in many people's lives and tends to show itself in consistent patterns. Let's then examine this pattern in terms of two people, one Eliza, the heroine of Pride and Prejudice and an instructor in the present times.

Each is presented with an opportunity and each responds in a similar way, indicating distinct patterns of response to the opportunity, matched by a difficult personal growth. The general phases in the process we have consistently witnessed when a great opportunity comes our way are in chronological order of occurrence:

1. Complete lack of awareness of the great opportunity.
2. Indifference when one finally does become conscious of the opportunity.
3. Hostility to the opportunity.
4. Recognition of the possible benefit of the opportunity.
5. A real positive response to the opportunity.
6. An impatience to gain the opportunity; even a desperation to gain it.
7. Experiencing physically and emotionally the full joy that the opportunity presents.
8. A recognition of one's faults and limitations that prevented one from ceasing the opportunity in the first place or being hostile to it (*i.e.,* one grows and evolves as a person).
9. Fully embracing the opportunity, though success at this point may be too later or diluted or if lucky

enough or deep enough change in one's attitudes and heart, full accomplishment.

In *Pride and Prejudice* Eliza aspires in her life to rise to a better position for herself and her family.

In 18th century England that usually occurred through marriage for a woman. Eliza is invited to a dance where the master of the estate Pemberley, Darcy, notices her. He is a very wealthy man (who she will later marry, which will vastly change her life for the better).

When he walks in the room she could care less. The result is that her first response to the approach of unprecedented opportunity is the typical response of people to what is far above their present level of accomplishment. She is completely unaware of the great opportunity.

Similarly in current times an instructor sees that other instructors are beginning to train on a few new programmes. He barely notices. The opportunity to go to a much higher level barely registers in his consciousness.

At the next stage (stage 2 as indicated above) in *Pride and Prejudice* Darcy asks Eliza to dance and she is completely indifferent. Likewise in our modern story when a programme manager asks the instructor if he is interested in attending a free train the trainer seminar on the new programme, he is indifferent.

At this stage when one becomes somewhat conscious of the opportunity, one reacts with indifference.

At the next (stage 3) Eliza through a series of events expresses her hostility to Darcy in her conversations with others. Likewise the instructor becomes anger with the training company that he would have to train on that new programme in an area far away where he would have to navigate through a lot of traffic every morning.

At this stage there is a stirring in their emotions as it relates to the opportunity and express their feelings about it or to related people or circumstance as hostility

At stage 4 Eliza speaks with other people and comes to realise that there actually may be real benefits to involvement with Darcy after all. Likewise, the instructor relents in his anger and recognises that teaching this new programme may not be so bad after all after he sees other's enthusiastic about it and express that it may lead to other benefits which can help their career financially and interest-wise. He sees the same for himself. At this stage they both experience through life experiences the benefit of taking up the opportunity.

At stage 5, both Eliza in 18th century England and the instructor in 20th century America begin to see the real benefit of the opportunity and begin to have the first full positive response to the opportunity.

Also, along the way there is also the beginnings of the recognition of their own limited beliefs and attitudes that prevented one from reacting positively to the opportunity in the first place. They recognised their own stupidity, arrogance and misplaced passions and energy, among others. (This recognition is in fact an indication of their personal growth and evolution).

At stage 6 one becomes impatient to undertake the opportunity; there is a lack of calm and perhaps even a sense of desperation. For Eliza it is an almost panic need to meet with Darcy. The instructor frantically tries calling the training manager (who is not in!) to attend a second train the trainer seminar on the software application.

At stage 7 each experience physically and emotionally the full joy that the opportunity presents. Eliza finally manages to visit Darcy's enormous estate and experiences the full physical pleasure of her walk around the estate, recognising that she could become its co-inhabitant. She has the full sensation of the great opportunity that has come her way. Likewise, the instructor attends the train-the-trainer seminar and experiences first hand the joy of learning that particular new programme.

At stage 8 there is a great recognition of one's past faults and limitations that prevented one from ceasing the opportunity in the first place. This is where the greatest personal growth comes in to play. For Eliza she realises how foolish she has been in getting involved with another man Wickham, who was a scoundrel. She also realises how foolish she has been in defending her family, including her very crude mother and her scandalous younger sister. She recognises her own responsibility in losing Darcy and her family's responsibility in her loss as well. She takes the attitude of fully acknowledging what she is.

Likewise the instructor comes face-to-face with his attitudes that led to his negative response to opportunities. He even thinks back and recognises other points in his life where he has had the same response, which also led to the devastation of other great possibilities.

At stage 9 one fully embraces the opportunity, though success at this point is not guaranteed in full or at all. In Eliza's case she releases her held, back emotions and confesses to him her lack of gratitude to Darcy (who has actually helped her family in many other ways which she only recently came to understand). Because of many other extenuating positive circumstances, they come together and marry.

The environment was supportive of their coming together despite all the twists and turns. On the other hand, in the case of the instructor, his opportunity is only partially gained. He does some training in that area, but has lost the real thrust of the opportunity.

We should mention that often there is one other factor that may lurk in the background. Often when a great opportunity presents itself to someone suddenly a negative force appears on the scene that tries to deny the accomplishment. *For Example,* in Eliza's case, though there is great opportunity for accomplishment through her marriage to Darcy, she is sidetracked by an infatuation with the scoundrel Wickham.

It is Eliza's eventual ability to recognise her weakness and through off Wickham's influence that puts her back on the right path. The positive atmosphere around her also gives support despite her foolish passions. Likewise, in the life of the instructor a difficulty arose in the form of a noisy and bullyish neighbour who he had a confrontation with, causing the instructor to be physically incapacitated for months.

In summary then when presented by great opportunities in life one often does not respond in full, which may lead one to have to traverse some or all of these nine plus stages so that one can come to terms with oneself (and thereby grow and evolve as a person) or accomplish or both. Of course, the more conscious we are in the first place the more we can react positively to the great opportunities that life presents.

By elevating our capacities and character through the many techniques outlined at this site (improving our attitudes, skills, energy, effort, direction, etc.), we can become the person who is more readily able to respond to the opportunities that life presents and accelerate accomplishment in life, rather than meandering through a maze of events and circumstance that causes us to grow through pain and eventually achieve.

INVOLUTION AND EVOLUTION

Our ability to accomplish great things in our lives are tied to our capacities and character, as well as to the challenges that life presents to us. These external challenges and circumstance bring us face-to-face with our character. Those who are able to understand their weaknesses and adjust are far more likely to succeed than those who do not. Those who change with life, grow and open the doors to greater accomplishment. One who learn from mistakes, changes bad attitudes and are open to opportunities that life presents are sure to open wide the doors of opportunity and accomplishment.

From a deeper level we can look at accomplishment from the perspective of the evolution of the individual. An individual has certain capacities and character. Against this backdrop life presents opportunities and challenges. The person who evolves his capacities and character accomplishes; the person who doesn't stays where he is even regresses. The circumstances that life presents and the our own capacities and characters are the starting point. This starting point is the "involution"; the basis from which we can evolve.

It is only natural that we would want only positive circumstances to occur in our lives. Yet it is a great irony of life that much of our individual growth and development comes about through the difficulties in our lives, *i.e.*, the involution. It is by overcoming our limited capacities and character playing out against difficult circumstances that we accomplish at greater levels.

For example, in the book Pride and Prejudice Darcy accomplishes at a higher level after he overcomes his limitations as a person. Through life's circumstances (the involution) he must overcome his arrogance as a rich, important aristocrat, which is only at the surface of his being. By overcoming his limitations against the play of difficult circumstances he comes to realise that he is in fact a good man.

This change of heart leads to Eliza being attracted to him, which leads to a great accomplishment in his life, their marriage. Equally great is that the process causes him to become a finer person, which can only lead to more meaningful accomplishment for him in the future. Through life's situations (the involution) he is forced to confront his nature, which he finally does (the evolution).

The involution provides the necessary foundation and circumstances for the evolution. Without it the person would remain the same, the force for accomplishment at a higher level would not be there.

All that we perceive as unconsciousness, opposition, obstacle, resistance, hostility and perversity–in others, the life around us and even in ourselves–are products of the involution that play essential roles in the emergence of positive characteristics and accomplished capacities in the evolution. Involution is the essential basis for the evolution

This process of evolution through the evolution is a process that individuals are going through. It also turns out to be the very same process which society itself is going through. If we examine social development we see that it to evolves by overcoming its limited capacities against a field of difficult situations.

If both individuals and society go through this process in a similar way it would suggest that perhaps life itself progresses in such a way. In fact, in his opus The Life Divine Sri Aurobindo, the Indian author and sage, suggests that life itself follow this process of evolution from out of the involution.

He goes back to the creation itself and describes how life emerged out in duality and falsehood. He suggests that from out of the Absolute, the Divine, (*i.e.*, the source of everything) emerged matter and life. The forms that were created were not perfect but were in fact were divided and false. This is the involution of creation. From that involution the forms struggle over time to create unity and truth, *i.e.*, the evolution.

In The Life Divine Sri Aurobindo describes the process of involution by which the One, infinite, indivisible, formless omnipresent and omniscient Reality, the Self-Conscious Being, creates out of itself a world of multiple, divided, ignorant, impotent forms and the process of evolution by which these forms struggle to survive, grow and rise in consciousness to manifest in form the infinite potentials of the formless reality.

Just as the universe struggles from out of its ignorance and falsehood, society and individuals do the same. Through the limitations of our nature and the forces surrounding, us we are confronted with our limitations (*i.e.,* the involution) so that out of this ignorance and falsehood we can progress and accomplish (the evolution). In other words we as individuals are participating in a process that the entire universe is going through.

Sri Aurobindo also points out that the Absolute itself in its creation of the universe is going through a process of accomplishment that parallels the process of accomplishment for society and the individual. In the process of creation (which is its form of accomplishment) the Absolute reveals a number of properties in that process of creation.

In the universe that came as a result of the creation those properties reveal themselves as determinants. These determinants are in us and reveal a parallel process that we go through when we try to accomplish.

OPTIMAL ACCOMPLISHMENT

What then is the key to the greatest accomplishment in life. We believe it is a combination of aspiration and values. One's aspiration for achievement, accomplishment, attainment, results, benefit, fulfilment of ideals and values is one great factor. The other is the strength and contents of one's personal values. Combining a great aspiration and fully formed and focused personal values, one can attain the peaks of efficiency and thereby achievement and accomplishment in life.

By efficiency we mean one is able to attain the greatest reward with the least effort. Great aspiration and high personal values tied to that aspiration, creates the greatest efficiency, which is the greatest accomplishment with the least effort.

Great aspiration and focused key values are then maximised in their ability to create results by our maximum efforts in life. Without our maximum efforts the aspirations and values will remain unfulfilled, the greater the effort, the more life will respond in kind. Tied to great aspiration and key values the results will be infinitely gratifying.

For those who aspire for something even greater; for the ultimate efficiencies to "move life" one can live the inner life, where one masters the forces of the world, around one's self from within one self. One can learn to shift from a life Centred on one's own individual ego sense and instead open to, surrender to the Higher Power, the Divine around us and use that Force as the basis of accomplishment.

By opening to that dimension, that Force, one opens to the infinite possibilities of accomplishment in life. He Higher Power's Creative action is a thousand times more efficient than our own individual effort. Opening to the Force through a process of consecrated effort, can bring in weeks what took a lifetime to attain; enables life to respond almost instantaneously. This is the greatest efficiency in life, which brings the greatest accomplishment with the least (outer) effort.

One needs to determine what is the best approach for that individual. Most can utilise aspiration and values. Some can rise to utilising the Force. Surely a combination of great aspiration; well developed, focused and utilised values making the full, maximum effort in life; and opening to the spiritual, divine force will lead to the ultimate and most efficient great, even infinite accomplishment, achievement, success and joy in life.

Things to Think About: Do you have a great aspiration for something in life. If not, why not; and what can you do about it? If yes, then is it being utilised and channelled through your own personal values. Do you have a set of key personal values that are the driving force in your life? What are they? If not, how can you develop such? How can you use a combination of great aspiration and key values to accomplish more in life? Come up with an action plan to see it through.

INNER TECHNIQUES

Calling the Force: Finally, we would like to mention the inner or spiritual techniques to help one accomplish in life. Many of us have resorted to prayer or meditation as a way to solve serious problems in our lives. Fewer of us however have actually adopted such a technique on a regular and ongoing basis, when things were not going particularly poorly or when things are going well. Utilising such techniques can bring about great fortune and joy in our lives.

For example, one powerful technique is something closely related to prayer. We call it "calling." Our experience is that if one were to take any situation and call the higher spiritual power into that situation life responds sooner or later in a very positive way. *For example,* you can use calling on a daily basis in your work:

> *The owner of a chain of audio-video stores in Canada took up the technique of calling. Whenever he went to one of his stores he called the higher presence into that location. Within a year of utilising this technique, profits increase six fold!*

Deference to Higher Source to Create Positive Circumstance: Spiritual consciousness has been felt from time immemorial as a force or current that uplift our spirits. In addition, that force can also be utilised to improve our daily lives.

Normally we create positive outcomes in our lives by having the right skills and knowledge, the proper level of organisation, the right attitudes and taking the necessary effort, amongst other. If we optimise our capacities, we are sure to meet with success and happiness in any activity or circumstance. Yet to move to a level of *perfection* in any situation or circumstance, we need one thing more; the cooperation of life.

In life we don't normally have any real control over external circumstance surrounding the event or circumstance we engage in, such as the occurrence of a sudden fire drill in the middle of a meeting we are conducting or a key person arriving late to the meeting because of a traffic incident. We don't have the ability to effect or prevent such things. Likewise, if we don't know the answer to a problem that we are suddenly confronted with, we don't know where to turn. The only thing we really seem to have control of is our *own* current capacities.

Then how can we truly become the master of any action, project, circumstance or situation we partake in? How do we overcome any barrier that appears beyond our control?

Our research indicates that you can gain this control by developing the simple discipline of remembering or deferring to the spiritual consciousness before the activity or event commences. By making this smallest of efforts you will experience that somehow life responds in a positive way.

For example, an engineer deferring to the spirit before beginning his work can have breakthrough discoveries or insights that he or she could never have been able to have based only on one's own knowledge, skills and efforts. An instructor who opens to the force before his class commences watches as everything during the day seems to dovetail perfectly into place and anticipated problems just vanish.

Deferring to the higher consciousness, the spirit, the Divine, if you will, opens us up to unlimited, even infinite possibilities, transcending the skills, knowledge, attitudes and other capacities we bring to the situation. Opening to this higher force before commencing an act has the power to evoke positive responses from life.

Actions are completed much better than expected, people respond more positively, events move more quickly and life "co-operates." This power solves problems, resolves conflicts, dissolves dead habits and unwanted traits, opens up new opportunities, generates freshness and enjoyment in everything we do, widens the personality, deepens our awareness and reveals one's true inner self. To experience this effect just *once* in one's life is to set one onto a new course in life.

Our experiences suggest this method of deference to a higher force before commencing an activity is a scientific, provable fact, witnessed thousands of times by our researchers, with *unprecedented* positive results. *If you try it and see the results once, it could change your life forever.*

❑

2

SKILLS FOR SUCCESS

The major focus of vocational training programmes is to teach people the skills necessary to accomplish job tasks. However, "life skills" are just as necessary for job success. Life skills constitute a continuum of knowledge and aptitudes that are necessary for a person to function independently and to avoid interruptions of the employment experience.

When one considers all of the skills that go into maintaining a job, it becomes clear that life skills are as important as job skills. Prior to going to work, a person must figure out what to wear, wash up, figure out what she is going to eat at breakfast and lunch and make sure she has transportation to get to work on time. Once at work, she needs to interact appropriately with her co-workers and supervisor, handle problems appropriately and understand her paycheck.

She needs to know how to budget that money wisely and engage in healthy, enjoyable activities outside of work. Major skill deficits in one or more of these areas could result in loss of job and require further training at a community rehabilitation programme. Without the resources to teach a person life skills, further job skill training could be a wasted effort.

In order to address this problem, Life Skills for Vocational Success has been developed. A life skills curriculum is not a novel concept. In many ways, this manual is not novel either. Like other products available, Life Skills for Vocational Success contains training materials in the typical areas of life skill training such as social skills, money management, employability and health. Furthermore, Life Skills for Vocational Success relies on common teaching strategies such as modelling and role-playing. Despite the similarities, this manual deviates from many other life skills training manuals in the following ways:

1. *Life Skills for Vocational Success* is specifically designed for employment success. It is assumed that people have participated in a training programme to learn daily living skills and become more independent. The training plans in this manual are devised to provide advanced training for those people who are preparing to go to work, but need further training to be successful on the job.
2. *Life Skills for Vocational Success* contains reviews and recommendations for using other life skills training materials available on the market.
3. *Life Skills for Vocational Success* contains lesson plans designed to teach a person skills rather than to provide general knowledge. It is too common for a training programme to present information and test the comprehension of that information using exercises like cross-word puzzles. It is important that students practise opening a checking account instead of finding the words "checking account" in a word find activity.
4. *Life Skills for Vocational Success* incorporates the benefits of the Internet in training life skills. In addition to providing a wealth of information on disabilities and vocational rehabilitation, it is a great resource for life skills information. Information on child care, buying a car, health care, insurance, etc., can be found on the Internet. As access to the Internet

becomes common for community rehabilitation programmes, trainers will be able to get information for training and teach students to get their own information to help them in their daily routine.

There are many wonderful training packages that use video, computer and other stimulating materials. The problem with these materials is that they are expensive and sometimes the usefulness is questionable. This manual includes recommendations about quality training materials and companies. For those organisations that cannot afford the best materials available, the curriculum is designed to provide solid training curricula independent of any product available on the market. This ensures that lack of resources will not keep people from the training they need.

In addition to providing curricula that is accessible to any programme, *Life Skills for Vocational Success* is designed to address the needs of people with varying strengths and deficits. Because this programme can not address all of these different needs, it is written to address the needs of the highest percentage of people who tend to have difficulty developing appropriate life skills. While this group is by no means homogenous, people with mental disabilities (retardation, mental illness, learning disability), a substance abuse history or life experiences that have interfered with the development of these skills will benefit most from this training.

The training is not designed to teach people basic reading, writing, math and communication skills. This does not mean that people who have severe deficits in these remedial skills can not benefit from the training. It just means that the life skills curriculum is not designed to provide that training. One might consider some of those skills as prerequisites for the training. The lessons are flexible enough for trainers to mold the information to the student's learning ability.

As mentioned previously, the lesson plans could not be developed to meet the needs of every person receiving vocational rehabilitation services, so it is designed to be flexible. This allows the trainer to fit the training to needs of the individual and the knowledge and expertise of the trainer. The lesson plans are not written in stone. Trainers will be able to provide effective training by following the format as written. If the information is too complex, trainers can simplify the information. If a student or group of students want more information, the trainer should look to the "Supplemental Resources" section of particular lessons that might be used to provide more information. The training will be effective if a trainer wants to make adaptations, utilise the recommended supplemental resources or incorporate a lesson into an already existing training programme.

OVERVIEW OF THE CURRICULUM

The *first* unit, *Social Skills,* provides training on standard social skills such as communication skills, anger management and conflict resolution. In addition, lessons are available on making friends and getting alongwith co-workers and roommates. Much of the training in this unit relies on practising the skills to help a person become more socially competent.

The *second* unit, *Decision-making Skills,* is short, but important. Problem-solving and decision-making skills are probably the most important skills a person can develop. Making good decisions and the ability to solve problems can make up for a lot of skill deficits. *For example,* a person may not know how to ride a bus to work, but the ability to solve problems may help him figure out who he needs to talk to in order to make sure he gets to work each day. This unit provides three different problem solving techniques.

Unit three, *Employability,* covers a wide range of skills that are necessary to retain a job. Because there are extensive resources on job readiness and job seeking available in print and on the Internet, trainers will find little information on obtaining a job. Lessons on getting to work on time, understanding standard procedures during the first few days on the job and wearing proper attire can assist students in getting off on the right foot on the job. A lesson on sexual behaviour in the work-place provides training in the areas of sexual harassment and dating co-workers. Other lessons in the unit provide an overview of standard expectations of employers regarding safety, productivity, attitude and acting appropriately.

Unit four, *Money Management*, has a little more complicated material due to the nature of the skills. As mentioned earlier, basic money handling skills will not be covered. The material has been simplified as much as possible while keeping enough information in the lesson to provide comprehensive training. Standard money management topics are included such as understanding the benefits of the job, budgeting, using a bank and using credit. Additional topics include protecting your money and staying out of debt.

Transportation is the fifth unit. Transportation covers a wide range of skills, from teaching someone to ride a bus in a step-by-step sequence to teaching someone about the process of buying a car. This unit addresses the fact that people in vocational rehabilitation settings have different skills and different financial means. A person who has limited financial resources and does not have the ability to drive would not be appropriate for training on owning a car. Training on using public transportation would be more appropriate. This unit provides an excellent example of how the training can be used to fit the needs of each individual.

Unit six, *Health*, provides training on maintaining a healthy lifestyle. There is a wealth of information on staying healthy. This unit gives students information that will help them avoid getting sick and perform well at work. Topics include fitness, nutrition, the problems of drug and alcohol use related to the job and accessing and using medical services appropriately. The unit contains a lesson on how to use sick leave benefits appropriately.

Unit seven, *Family Responsibilities*, provides necessary information about pregnancy, securing child care and how to balance working with the responsibilities of caring for a sick, elderly or disabled family member.

Basic Understanding of the Law is the unit eight. This unit covers information that many students need to stay out of trouble at work and in society. The unit also contains information about hiring a lawyer. A final area of focus is understanding and using the laws of the Americans with Disabilities Act to receive necessary accommodations at work, in public buildings and while using public transportation.

The last unit, *Telephone Skills*, provides basic training on obtaining phone numbers, getting information over the phone and using proper phone manners when looking for a job and while on the job. There is also a lesson on making long distance phone calls. The appendices contain information in four basic areas. *First*, there are several appendices that contain government documents used in the training.

Second, appendix I contains reviews of educational materials on the market. Due to the cost of ordering preview copies, a few products from each company were ordered to get a sampling of the overall quality of the products. Any product that was received was reviewed and a summary and recommendation for use can be found in this section.

Due to the enormous cost of some of these products, it is impractical for any one agency to purchase the materials necessary to put together a well-rounded curriculum. There are some comprehensive life skill packages available, but they tend to very expensive. Some materials cost ₹ 44.33 thousands or more. The resource directory is intended to provide the reader a review of the materials so he/she can make a more informed decision.

Third, appendix I includes companies that sell life skills training products. Although this list is not comprehensive, it will provide trainers a list of companies to contact if they are interested in obtaining a catalogue to purchase life skill educational materials.

THE ASSERTIVENESS

- *Eye Contact:* Make sure the person is more interesting than what is on the floor. Look at the person most of the time. But do not stare at people 100 percent of the time.
- *Body Posture:* Try to face the person. Stand or sit up tall. But, don't be a stiff board.
- *Distance/Physical Contact:* If you smell or feel the other person's breath, you are probably too close. Keep a comfortable distance.
- *Gestures:* Use hand gestures to add to what you are saying, but remember that you are not conducting an orchestra.
- *Facial Expressions:* Your face should match your emotion and what you are saying. Don't laugh when you are upset and don't have a frown when you are happy. A relaxed, pleasant face is best when you are happy. A relaxed, serious face is best when you are upset.
- *Voice Tone, Inflection, Volume:* When you are making an assertive message, you want to be heard. In order to be heard you have to pay attention to the tone of your voice (happy, whiny, upset), the inflection of your voice (emphasis on syllables) and volume of your voice (whisper to yell).
- *Fluency:* It is important to get out your words in an efficient manner. If a person stammers or rambles on, the listener gets bored.

- *Timing:* When you are expressing negative feelings or making a request of someone, this is especially important. Seven days later may be too long. Doing it right on the spot in front of people may not be the right time to do it. Do it as soon as there is a time for both parties to resolve their issues alone.
- *Listening:* An important part of assertiveness. If you are making statements that express your feelings without infringing on the rights of others, you need to give the other person a chance to respond.
- *Content:* What a person says is one of the most important parts of the assertive message. Depending on what a person is trying to accomplish, the content is going to be different.

SOCIAL SKILLS

Objectives

1. Identify the differences between good body language and bad body language during conversation.
2. Identify the differences between good body language and bad body language when taking instructions or receiving criticism from a supervisor.
3. Practise good body language during a conversation.
4. Practise good body language while a supervisor is giving instructions or criticising.

Instructional Format: This topic will mainly involve modelling and role-playing. Begin the lesson by talking about the importance of how one looks on the outside during interactions with others. If a person looks uninterested during a conversation, he will have a hard time making and keeping friends. If a person looks angry or annoyed when her boss tells her to do something, her boss may think she has a bad attitude. It is helpful to video-tape role-plays. If you have the equipment, it is highly recommended.

1. Model both bad and good body language during a conversation. Have the students try to identify whether you have good or bad body language. Good body language involves keeping good personal space, making eye contact, sitting or standing up straight and looking interested. When you are doing the bad role-play, do only one thing wrong (stare at the floor, turn body side-ways, scowl, fidget, rock back and forth, cross arms, slouch, etc.) and see if the students can identify what you are doing wrong.
2. Model both bad and good body language when a supervisor is giving instructions or criticising.
3. Instruct students on good body language during conversation and when supervisors are giving orders. Have the students practise the skills in role-plays. The components of good body language during spoken communication mainly involve not doing the bad things mentioned above. But, it is important to talk about the following:
   - *Eye Contact:* Look at the person the majority of the time.
   - *Keep Still:* Don't fidget, rock back and forth, play with hair or clothes.
   - *Personal Space:* It is hard to talk when you are 10 feet apart, but you do not want to be 6 inches apart either. Generally, 2-3 feet is a comfortable distance for most people.
   - *Posture:* Sitting-up straight or even leaning toward the speaker lets the person know you are interested. When you slouch, it is not showing good manners and it tells the speaker that you are more interested in relaxing or may be falling asleep than listening to her.

Communication Skills

Objectives

1. Identify the skills of active listening.
2. Practise the skills during role-play situations.

Instructional Format: This topic will mainly involve modelling and role-playing. Use the lesson on body language to reinforce the information taught in this topic. Remind the students that effective listening takes practise and effort. There are going to be times when a person does not feel like listening. Inform her that it is probably more courteous to inform the speaker that it is not a good time to talk rather than to pretend to listen. However, on a job site, a person may not have that option and will need to use all of her energy to listen to a supervisor or co-worker. It is helpful to video-tape role-plays. If you have the equipment, it is highly recommended.

1. Ask the participants to list skills that are necessary for effective listening. Use the handout, "Keys to Effective Listening," to aid in the discussion. Make sure to cover each of the major points.
2. Model both bad and good listening skills during role-play conversations. The conversations can be about the weather, sports, what is going on at work, what people are going to do on the weekend or did last weekend, etc.
3. Students should role-play conversations using the skills of effective listening. There are some activities that could be used to practise the skills beyond the role-plays. These activities may not be appropriate for all students, depending on their functioning level. Trainers should use their judgement in what activities are appropriate for what classes.

- One activity is to give the learner a set of instructions to complete something. This is a good way to test listening and comprehension skills. One skill that can be employed when giving instructions to lower functioning individuals is self-instructional training. Self-instruction training requires the listener to repeat what is said as a way to remember the instructions. Initially, the student says the steps out loud. Following practise, the student hopefully will be able to say the instructions in her head. The instructions and activity should be modified for different learning, cognitive and or physical abilities. Activities should involve two or more steps. *For example,* **(1)** pick up the pen, **(2)** go over to the table where the paper is and **(3)** write your name. Or, **(1)** Go to that table, **(2)** pick up the ball, **(3)** bounce it three times and **(4)** put it back on the table.

- A second activity is to do the "gossip" game in which a person tells one person a short story (three to four sentences that are written down), the listener then whispers the story to his neighbour and this continues until the last person tells the story out loud. The object is to see how much the story is changed in the translation. Do this activity. To demonstrate the benefits of effective listening, do the same activity but have the participants use good listening skills rather than just whispering into each others' ears. For the purpose of this exercise, the leader will take one person out of the room or away from the group and tell a different story. This will allow the speaker and listener to use good skills instead of whispering the story in each other's ear. Once the story is told, the leader calls another student away from the group and observes while the previous listener tells the new person the story. This should continue until all students get a chance to listen. If the group is too big, stop the activity after about five to ten minutes. Gather the whole group together and have the last listener tell the story. The trainer should read the original story so the class can compare. The complexity of the story should be altered depending on the cognitive abilities of the students.

- A third activity is a version of "Simon Says." During the first round, have the students face away from "Simon" and look at a TV. During the second round, they look at "Simon" and can repeat the instructions (self-instructional training). Discuss whether the students followed directions better the second time around.

❑

3

DYNAMISM AND ENTHUSIASM

Failure can knock the confidence and enthusiasm out of people as quickly and as easily as a punch on the nose can make your eyes water. How can we recover and maintain the enthusiasm we have lost? How can we learn to see clearly once more?

Only a few years ago, I attended a seminar organised by the Anthony Robbins group on making money through investing in shares amongst other things.

As I walked out of the doors full of enthusiasm and excitement ready to make the most of my new-found confidence and knowledge, I was met by men in straw hats who were advertising a course on making money through investing in shares. I attended the weekend course and my enthusiasm and confidence increased. A year or so later I had managed to lose ₹ 21.20 lakhs after being conned by some share brokers who turned out to be criminal fraudsters. They were 'selling' shares they did not own.

My lazy failure to check them out was more to blame than the seminar and course but my enthusiasm and excitement vanished like snow in the morning sun.

I have been on an investment course since but my enthusiasm is still gone. By losing enthusiasm, I have added one failure to another and have not followed the great advice of Winston Churchill:

"Success is going from failure to failure without a loss of enthusiasm."

After losing money, I should have 'climbed back on the horse' as it were and invested what little I had left. Maybe I will one day. In the mean time I have focussed on internet marketing instead and am gradually making progress in that field and despite some setbacks have maintained my enthusiasm.

I was impressed, yesterday, by reading Jason Cox's blog. Jason is a very successful and very young internet entrepreneur. He described a list of projects he had undertaken in 2005.

Some of them–the ones he had created himself–were complete flops but the copycat projects were a huge success. He had maintained his enthusiasm throughout. He did not allow the flops to stop his momentum or quench his enthusiasm. Success follows that kind of attitude like rivers follow rain.

Another great quote by Paul J. Meyer sums up his attitude:

> *"Whatever you vividly imagine, ardently desire, sincerely believe and enthusiastically act upon must inevitably come to pass!"*

This quote hints at the secrets of maintaining our enthusiasm. We need to vividly imagine our eventual success as if it was already ours. We need to fan our desire by thinking about why we are following this particular dream. We need to believe that we have the ability to achieve our goals and we need to act with enthusiasm.

If we don't feel enthusiastic, we need to act as if we do and the feeling will often follow on. We need to climb back on the horse if we fall off and not lie complaining on the grass.

The original meaning of enthusiasm means 'God in you'. With God in us, we should be capable of performing miracles or, at least, extraordinary deeds.

If we can maintain our enthusiasm instead of losing it when we fail, we should end up in the land of miracles and the land of the extraordinary.

FORGING SELF-CONFIDENCE

What you know and what you don't know is critical to your success in all walks of life. A young woman wrote to me recently, telling me that her whole life had taken a different turn since she heard me ask the question, "What one great thing would you dare to dream if you knew you could not fail?"

She wrote that, up to that time, this was a question she had never even dared to consider, but now, she thought of nothing else. She had realised, in a great, blinding flash of clarity, that the main thing separating her from her hopes and dreams was the belief in her ability to achieve them.

Most of us are like this for most of our lives. There are many things that we want to be and have and do, but we hold back. We are unsure because we lack the confidence necessary to step out in faith in the direction of our dreams.

Abraham Maslow said that the story of the human race is the story of men and women "selling themselves short." Alfred Adler, the great psychotherapist, said that men and women have a natural tendency towards feelings of inferiority and inadequacy.

Because we lack confidence, we don't think we have the ability to do the kind of things that others have done and in many cases, we don't even try.

Just Think: What difference would it make in your life if you had an absolutely unshakable confidence in your ability to achieve anything you really put your mind to? What would you want and wish and hope for? What would you dare to dream if you believed in yourself with such deep conviction that you had no fears of failure whatsoever?

Most people start off with little or no self-confidence, but as a result of their own efforts, they become bold and brave and outgoing. And we've discovered that if you do the same things that other self-confident men and women do, you, too, will experience the same feelings and get the same results.

The key is to be true to yourself, to be true to the very best that is in you and to live your life consistent with your highest values and aspirations.

Take some time to think about who you are and what you believe in and what is important to you. Decide that you will never compromise your integrity by trying to be or say or feel something that is not true for you.

Have the courage to accept yourself as you really are–not as you might be or as someone else thinks you should be and know that, taking everything into consideration, you are a pretty good person. After all, we all have our own talents, skills and abilities that make us extraordinary.

No one, including yourself, has any idea of your capabilities or of what you might ultimately do or become. Perhaps the hardest thing to do in life is to accept how extraordinary you really can be and then to incorporate this awareness into your attitude and personality.

In developing unshakable levels of self-confidence, your self-esteem and self-regard are important starting points, but they are not enough. People have tried positive thinking and wishing and hoping for years, with only mixed results.

To develop the deep-down kind of self-confidence that leads to victory, you need positive knowing, not just positive thinking.

Lasting self-confidence really comes from a sense of control. When you feel very much in control of yourself and your life, you feel confident enough to do and say the things that are consistent with your highest values.

Psychologists today agree that a feeling of being "out of control" is the primary reason for stress and negativity and for feelings of inferiority and low self-confidence. And the way for you to get a solid sense of control over every part of your life is to set clear goals or objectives, to establish a sense of direction based on purposeful behaviour aimed at predetermined ends.

Being true to yourself means knowing exactly what you want and having a plan to achieve it. Lasting self-confidence comes when you absolutely know that you have the capacity to get from where you are to wherever you want to go.

You are behind the wheel of your life. You are the architect of your destiny and the master of your fate.

Instead of being preoccupied with the fear of failure and loss, as most people are, you focus on the opportunity and the possible gains of achievement.

With a clearly-defined track to run on, you become success-oriented and you gradually build your confidence up to the stage where there is very little you will not take on.

Another essential way to build your self-confidence, through positive knowing rather than just positive thinking, is to become very good at what you do. The flip side of self-confidence is "self-efficacy," or the ability to perform effectively in your chosen area.

You can raise your self-confidence instantly by the simple act of committing yourself to becoming excellent in your chosen field. You immediately separate yourself from the average individual who drifts from job to job and accepts mediocrity as the adequate standard.

Some years ago, a young man named Tim came to one of my personal-development seminars. He was shy and introverted. His handshake was weak and he had tremendous difficulty in making eye contact. He sat in the back of the seminar room with his head down, taking notes. He seemed to have few friends and he didn't socialise very much during the breaks.

At the end of the seminar, he told me that he was in sales and hadn't been doing very well up to that time. But he had resolved to change, to go to work on himself, to overcome his shyness and to become very good at selling for his company. He then said good-bye and I wished him the best of luck as he went on his way.

A year later, he came back to take the seminar again. But this time, he was distinctly different. He was calmer and more self-assured. He was still a little shy, but when he shook hands, his grip was firmer and his eye contact was better. He sat toward the middle of the seminar room and he interacted quietly with people around him.

At the end of the seminar, he told me that he was starting to move up in his sales force and had his best year ever. He was determined to do even better in the year to come.

About 14 months later, Tim came back to the seminar. This time, he brought five people from his company, all of whom he had convinced to come to the seminar and he had offered to pay their tuition if they weren't satisfied.

He walked right up to me and shook hands firmly, looking me straight in the eye with a strong, self-confident smile. He asked if I remembered him and I told him that I remembered him very well. He said that he had brought something that he wanted to show me.

He took out of his pocket a letter from the president of a national corporation–one of the biggest companies in the country–personally congratulating him for the outstanding job he had done in sales in his territory in the past year.

It turned out that Tim had gone from number 33 to number one out of 42 sales-people. His income had risen from ₹ 11.52 lakhs a year to ₹ 43.44 lakhs and he had increased his sales volume at a faster rate than any other salesperson in the country had.

He was still quiet, but he had a wonderful air of power and purposefulness about him. He had taken the steps and paid the price to build himself into a fine young man.

He had made the decision to do whatever was necessary to overcome his shyness and to develop the kind of personality that he admired in others. He was and is, in every sense of the word, a self-made man.

Perhaps the most wonderful result of developing high levels of self-confidence is the positive impact that your personality will have on your relationships.

There are two mental laws that are always operating and that determine much of what happens to you in your interactions with people.

The *first* is the law of attraction, which says that you will inevitably attract into your life people who are very much like you.

The *second* law is the law of correspondence, which says that your outer world of relationships will correspond perfectly, like a mirror image, to your inner world of personality and temperament.

In combination, these laws simply say that as you change in a positive direction, you will find yourself surrounded by people who are very much like the new person you are becoming.

As you get better, the quality and quantity of your relationships will get better. You will meet nicer, more self-confident, more interesting and enjoyable people.

You will find yourself getting along better with members of the opposite sex, including your spouse.

You will find yourself doing better at your job or even in a new job and getting along better with your boss and your co-workers.

Your attitude of confidence and calm assurance will make you more attractive to people. They will want to be around you, to open doors for you, to make opportunities available to you that would not have arisen when you didn't feel as terrific about yourself as you do now.

Often, people lack self-confidence in their relationships with others because they judge themselves poorly in comparison. Sometimes you become self-conscious of what you are doing and saying and sometimes you are afraid that people will not like you or accept you the way you want them to.

Well, there is an important mindset that you can adopt to improve your ability to get along well with others in a more relaxed and confident fashion.

It's important to remember that no one can affect your thoughts or feelings unless there is something that you want from him or something that you want him to refrain from doing.

As soon as you begin to practise detachment and decide in your own mind that there is nothing that you want or expect from another person, you will find that his ability to shake your self-confidence is greatly reduced.

The people who are the most successful in human relationships are those who practise a calm, healthy detachment from others and although they are friendly and engaged in the conversation, they don't allow the behaviours of others to determine how they think and feel about themselves.

As you can see, it is our fears and doubts that, more than anything else, undermine our self-esteem and self-confidence and cause us to think in negative terms about ourselves and our possibilities.

As Maslow said, we begin to "sell ourselves short" and see all the reasons why something might not be possible for us. We magnify the difficulties and minimise the opportunities. We become pre-occupied with the possible losses we might suffer and the possible criticisms we might endure.

Our fears and doubts paralyse us, preventing us from acting boldly, lowering our self-confidence and causing us to think and talk in negative terms. In fact, this probably describes the great majority of mankind.

Most people are so pre-occupied with their fears that they have time for little else and this pre-occupation manifests itself in much of what they say and do.

The only real antidote to doubt and worry and fear and all the other negative emotions that sabotage our self-confidence is action.

Your conscious mind can hold only one thought at a time, positive or negative. When you engage in systematic, purposeful action, using and stretching your abilities to the maximum, you cannot help but feel positive and confident about yourself.

Act as though it were impossible to fail. Act as though you already had a high level of self-confidence.

And continually ask yourself, "What one great thing would I dare to achieve if I knew I could not fail?" Whatever your answer, you can have it if you can dream it and if you have the self-confidence to go out and get it.

REMOVING NEGATIVE THOUGHTS

The question people often ask me is–when their self-development work and personal growth finally "takes," is this when will they stop having negative thoughts–I wish I knew. Although I'm afraid the answer could be never.

I play CDs with positive subliminal messages while I sleep each night. I start each day by reading something positive and end each night the same way. I have many positive, success-oriented people in my life. I feast regularly on positive books, tapes and other programmes.

But I have an embarrassing confession to make...

I've had lots of negative thoughts. Sometimes ten a day. As rich, successful, healthy and happy as I've become, I have often still had fear-based thoughts. Looking back now, I see a lot of things I did, thinking they were prosperous, but I see now they were fear-based.

When I bought a bike, I bought a titanium professional race bike for ₹ 1.32 lakhs. I remember thinking then that if things got bad, I could always sell it for some quick cash.

Well I bought three Vipers at the same time, I felt secure, knowing I could always sell one or two and scrape together a hundred grand.

Coming from the place I did, I always felt like I was somehow cheating destiny. That God or the universe or someone was going to wake up one day and discover that I had acquired wealth by mistake.

I still had that niggling thought in the back of my mind– the defensive, better-prepare-for-the-really-bad-scenario and have my options covered just in case. And not get my hopes up too high, because then I was setting myself up for a great disappointment.

And like I told you, I've had those kinds of thoughts recently, as many as ten a day. But here's the difference...

I notice every one of them now. Immediately. And I often laugh about how silly they are. Best of all, I see the progression of my mindset.

First, I had hundreds of negative thoughts a day and noticed none of them.

Then I graduated to the point that I had lots of negative thoughts a day and noticed some of them.

From there I got to the point that I had less negative thoughts a day and I noticed a lot of them.

And gradually over time, I started having less and less of them. Some days I have none. And now when I do have them, I catch myself right away.

I used to wear a rubber band on my wrist and snap it when I had a lack thought. Now I no longer need to do that. I just tap my fingers on my forehead. That's the signal to my mind and I instantly reject that thought and replace it with another one. And once that happens. The world changes.

So when do the negative thoughts end? I doubt they ever do. The sheer enormity of how much negative and lack programming you will be assaulted with over the course of a lifetime makes that seem unlikely. (But let's not affirm that.)

In any event, if you keep counter programming, you will win the fight. Because once you control the programming, you control the mindset. And once you control the mindset, you control your destiny!

Start a life journal and track your negative lack and limitation thoughts and tally them. At the end of each day, spend some time thinking about this subject.

When you really analyse the day and think about this regularly you will start to notice these thoughts. And once you do that, they lose most of their power.

And your mindset starts to change...

You change your core fundamental beliefs. You believe you are supposed to be healthy, happy and prosperous. You believe you are worthy. And when you are confronted with dozens of situations each day, most minor, some bigger and even some that are major, you expect good things to happen to you!

And because you expect good things to happen to you-you approach life differently. You approach it expecting to end up on top. And because you believe it, that's exactly what happens! Ain't it great?

HOW TO CHANGE YOUR LIFE?

Spend a moment contemplating deeply what I'm going to say, because I think it is very important. It is, in fact, often the biggest stumbling block people have in their attempts to become happier, more successful and more peaceful.

I often receive letters or e-mails from people who are unhappy and desperately want to change something in their life. Sometimes they want to end a chronic and negative emotional state that has taken over, such as anxiety, depression, fear or anger.

Sometimes they are experiencing one drama or crisis after another and cannot seem stop this cycle.

Sometimes it is a substance abuse problem or a problem of being in and staying in an abusive situation.

Sometimes it is a lack of money or personal success or an inability to create what they want in the world.

Whatever it is, these people write asking for my suggestions. I write back and tell them what I think.

In response to my suggestions, I often hear back from them something like this: "I tried that. It isn't me." Or, "I read that book and there wasn't anything in it that resonated with me." Or, they say: "I can't, because ...." Sometimes they say, "It's just my nature to be (fill in the blank)." Or, "That goes against my values, beliefs (or whatever)."

At that point, we get down to brass tacks, because now I really begin to understand what the problem is.

It's that they think they're going to stay the way they are, continue to think the way they think, continue to act the way they act and yet somehow their problem is going to change or go away!

So let's get really clear about one fundamental truth about life and about change if you continue to think the way you are thinking now and continue to act the way you are acting now, you will continue to get the same results you are getting now.

There are no exceptions to this.

The life you are leading–the amount of success you enjoy, the amount of money you make, the kind and quality of your personal relationships, the amount of pain or pleasure in your life, the amount of drama and crisis or stability and inner peace, in your life, the amount of emotional pain or emotional balance you experience–are all the direct result of how you think and how you act.

They are not the result of your environment, other people, luck, the alignment of the planets or the telepathic mind control techniques of evil aliens.

This means that if you want to change your circumstances and your results in life, you must change how you think and how you act. If you are determined to continue thinking and acting in the same way, resign yourself to getting the same results, because (trust me) that is what will happen.

So how do you know what changes to make in how you think and act? Find out how other people who are getting the results you want are thinking and acting and copy what they are doing.

If you think and act in the same way as people who are getting the kinds of results you want, you will get those results too. This always works.

The problem comes from your resistance to doing it. I get many letters from people who complain of lack of material resources, for instance, but when I suggest thinking and acting like those who are making a lot of money, they tell me they can't.

Making money isn't spiritual, they say or it exploits people or they don't have the energy or they aren't smart enough or whatever. If that's what you think, you're right, you will never become prosperous, because prosperous people do not have those beliefs.

To be prosperous, you must find out what prosperous people believe and adopt those beliefs. You must find out what their values are and adopt them. You must find out what their internal strategies for making decisions are and adopt them. And so on.

Unless you accidentally trip over buried treasure or win the lottery (I know some of you actually think you will), there is no other way to become prosperous than to adopt the beliefs, values, attitudes and mental strategies of prosperous people and then take action in the same way prosperous people take action.

The same can be said for creating inner peace, creating loving relationships or any other desirable outcome. Find out how those who are already doing it have constructed their inner map of reality and adopt the same inner map for yourself. Then, take the same actions. If you do this, you will succeed.

If you insist on keeping your beliefs, values, strategies and the other aspects of your map of reality and just cannot get yourself to adopt those of the people who are creating what you want to create, then be prepared to continue getting the same results you've been getting, because that's what is going to happen.

Your life results follow directly from how you think and act and there is no getting around this. How to do you find out what the people you want to model believe, value and so on? How do you learn their strategies and actions?

You can find this information from books or from people in person. You can find it on audio cassettes. If you look for it, it is all around you.

This book provides you with huge clues in how to do this. I'm particularly trying to paint a very clear picture of all the aspects of how people do the "think" part of thinking and acting, but I also throw in some of the "action" part from time to time as well. The only thing that is keeping most people from getting what they want in life is that they haven't yet figured out that:

(1) Whatever results you get in life flow from how you think and act and

(2) To change your results you must change how you do these two things.

If you like your current results, great. If not, you now know what to do.

Finally, using the centre point programme helps this process immeasurably because it creates increased conscious awareness, increased ability to watch yourself create whatever it is you are creating in your life.

As you watch and become more aware, those parts of your way of thinking and acting that do not serve you begin to fall away and are replaced by more resourceful ways of living.

If you are consciously modelling those who are creating what you want to create, it only accelerates the process. Becoming more conscious causes everything to fall into place. So keep listening to those Holosync soundtracks (or get in the programme if you're still procrastinating).

Anyone who is still breathing can change how they think and act and get any result they want in life, whether material, emotional, physical or spiritual–including you.

So what are you waiting for?

POSITIVE ATTITUDE

When I was 21 years old, a friend of mine and I decided to go off to see the world. Many of our friends were going to Europe and hitchhiking around with rucksacks. We decided to be different and go to Africa instead.

It never occurred to us to ask why no one else was going to Africa. We found that out later, much to our great regret, to get to our destination in Africa, we had to cross the Sahara Desert. Starting from London, we rode bicycles across France and Spain. The labour was excruciating, the progress was slow and the pleasure was non-existent.

In Gibraltar, we sold our bicycles and invested our last few dollars in an old Land Rover. We crossed from Gibraltar to Tangier and made our way through Morocco, over the Atlas Mountains and into Algeria.

We were on our way in Africa. Still, there was one obstacle between us and the greenery we were anxious to see and it was that darn, old desert.

Our Land Rover broke down many times, but we finally got it repaired and set off to cross the Sahara. We had no idea how serious and how difficult this adventure was to be.

As we moved south across the desert, we encountered endless problems, any one of which could have finished our trip and, probably, our lives. It was during this desert crossing that I learned one of the most important lessons in my life about attitude.

The French, who had controlled Algeria for many years, had marked a path across the desert with black, 55-gallon oil drums. The drums were spaced exactly five kilometres apart.

As we drove and came to an oil drum, the next drum, which was five kilometres ahead, would pop up on the horizon and the last oil drum, which was five kilometres behind, would fall off the horizon, as if shot in a shooting gallery.

Wherever we were, we could always see two oil drums at a time–the one we had just left and the one we were headed toward.

To cross one of the greatest deserts in the world, all we had to do was to take it "one oil barrel at a time." We did not have to cross the entire desert at once. We had to cross it only one oil barrel at a time and that would be sufficient.

For me, the Sahara crossing was a metaphor for life. In order to maintain a Positive Mental Attitude under all circumstances, all you really have to do is to take it one step, one oil barrel, at a time.

As Thomas Carlyle said, "Our great business is not to see what lies dimly at a distance, but to do what lies clearly at hand."

A Positive Mental Attitude is indispensable to success and achievement. You can build and maintain a Positive Mental Attitude by focusing on doing what lies clearly at hand, by taking the step that appears immediately in front of you.

That will automatically lead to the next step and the next and so on and eventually, you will find yourself at your goal.

But there is much more to a Positive Mental Attitude than this. You can have a positive attitude that immediately disappears in the face of adversity or you can have an attitude that is so strong that no matter what happens to you, you are able to remain positive, cheerful and optimistic.

The factor of self-confidence is what determines how positive your attitude really is. And self-confidence is based on your belief in yourself and your ability.

It is based on faith or knowing that things are going to work out well in the long run, no matter how distressing they appear to be in the short run.

Let me give you an example. A friend of mine was called by the Internal Revenue Service and told that he was to be the subject of a tax audit. The IRS officer wanted all his tax receipts and returns for the past three years brought in for examination.

My friend's first reaction was panic. He immediately became anxious and afraid of all the things that could happen.

However, he caught himself and began to apply his mind to keep his attitude calm and positive. First of all, he thought: Have I done anything that is unacceptable under the existing tax law? As he thought, he realised that he had made every effort to file accurate tax returns.

He then asked himself who else should be involved in the audit. As he thought, he realised that his accountant, who had prepared his tax returns, should be involved in explaining them. Now he was calm and collected.

He phoned his accountant and apprised him of the situation. The accountant explained to him that every year, the IRS audits a certain percentage of tax returns at random.

The fact that the IRS had chosen to audit him had nothing to do with whether or not his returns were accurate. It was simply routine procedure. The accountant also explained that if my friend wanted to send him, the accountant, to the meeting with the IRS agent, my friend didn't need to appear.

Now my friend was completely relaxed. He gathered the necessary documents and turned them over to his accountant, who had ample experience in dealing with the IRS. The accountant sat down with the IRS agent and went through everything, from beginning to end.

When it was over, the IRS agent thanked the accountant and said that, based on the tax returns, everything was in perfect order and there would be no need for a reassessment or for any additional payments or penalties. The audit was over and life went on.

Right from the beginning, you can choose to be positive and constructive in dealing with any adversity. You can sit down and think through the situation and then begin to deal with it one oil barrel at a time.

Of course, this isn't as easy as it sounds. We are all faced with four obstacles that tend to get in the way of our maintaining a Positive Mental Attitude. These obstacles are fear, worry, anger and doubt.

When things are not working out the way we had expected, our immediate response is to become fearful and uneasy. We are afraid that we will lose our money, waste our effort or forfeit our emotional or physical investment in what we have done.

If we are not careful, we start thinking of our potential losses rather than focusing on our potential gains.

Fear triggers worry and we begin to use our power of imagination to create all sorts of fanciful but negative images that cause us unhappiness and insomnia and make us unable to perform effectively.

Fear and worry create anger or what has been called the "victim complex." Instead of moving constantly forward in the direction of our dreams, we begin to react and respond and to blame other people and other situations for our problems.

Surrounding these negative emotions is the mental quality of doubt. Doubt forms the fertile breeding grounds for the other negative emotions.

Therefore, to eliminate these obstacles to positive thinking, you need to systematically use your mind to get rid of the weakening emotion of doubt.

How do you do this? It is simple. The only real antidote to fear, worry, anger and doubt is positive action toward the achievement of some worthwhile ideal.

Psychologists tell us that the key to dealing effectively with life is what they call the "cognitive control method." The cognitive control method says that you can really think about and concentrate on, only one thing at a time, either positive or negative.

Successful people are no different from you or me. They have one outstanding characteristic, however. They consciously choose to think about what they want, rather than what they don't want.

And, as a result, they are continuously taking action toward their goals, rather than spending their time thinking and worrying about the inevitable challenges and difficulties that face them every day.

Dr. Karl Pribram, the respected neuropsychologist, has found that human beings have holistic mental pictures stored within their brains. His discovery was that the "law of attraction" is alive and well and working within the mind of every human being.

Dr. Pribram discovered that any visual image, imagined in complete detail, sets-up a force field of energy that begins to attract into your life the people, ideas, things and even circumstances that are consistent with that image.

If you visualise a positive outcome, if you think about it and see it and feel it and sense it in every respect, you begin to exert a powerful magnetic force that brings the desired goal or outcome into reality.

In effect, you control your life and your destiny by the vivid mental images that you hold in your mind on a continuous basis. You are the architect of your personality and character.

Your goal, your desire, is to be as successful, happy and prosperous as you possibly can be in every aspect of your life. Therefore, the systematic and purposeful development of a Positive Mental Attitude is something that you need to work on every hour.

There are six things you can do to assure that your attitude is the very best it can be under all circumstances.

First: Whatever challenges you face, focus on the future rather than on the past. Instead of worrying about who did what and who is to blame, focus on where you want to be and what you want to do.

Get a clear mental image of your ideal successful future and then take whatever action you can to begin moving in that direction. As the New Testament says, "Let the dead bury the dead."

Let the past take care of itself and get your mind, your thoughts and your mental images on the future.

Second: Whenever you're faced with a difficulty, focus on the solution rather than on the problem. Think and talk about the ideal solution to the obstacle or setback, rather than wasting time rehashing and reflecting on the problem.

Solutions are inherently positive, whereas problems are inherently negative. The instant that you begin thinking in terms of solutions, you become a positive and constructive human being.

Third: Assume that something good is hidden within each difficulty or challenge. Dr. Norman Vincent Peale, a major proponent of positive thinking, once said, "Whenever God wants to give us a gift, he wraps it up in a problem."

The bigger the gift you have coming, the bigger the problem you will receive. But the wonderful thing is that if you look for the gift, you will always find it.

Fourth: Assume that whatever situation you are facing at the moment is exactly the right situation you need to ultimately be successful. This situation has been sent to you to help you learn something, to help you become better, to help you expand and grow.

One of the affirmations I have learned to use continually is this: "Every situation is a positive situation if I view it as an opportunity for growth and self-mastery." That is a wonderful affirmation. You cannot say it without thinking positive thoughts, feeling positive emotions and seeing positive actions that you can take.

Fifth: In every challenge, look for the valuable lesson. Assume that every setback contains a lesson that is essential for you to learn. Only when you learn this lesson will you be smart enough and wise enough to go on to achieve the big goals that you have set for yourself.

Again, since you can think about only one thing at a time, if you are busy looking for the lesson, you cannot simultaneously think about the difficulty or the obstacle. And, surprise, surprise, you will always find the lesson, if you look for it.

Sixth: The sixth way to keep your mind positive all the time is to make a list. Whenever you have a goal that is unachieved, a difficulty that is unresolved or a problem that is blocking you from getting where you want to go, sit down with a pen and paper and make a list of every single thing that you could possibly do to resolve the situation.

The more you think on paper, the more you will take control over your conscious mind. When you are writing down possible solutions, your mind will be positive, all the time.

As you write, you are taking advantage of the power of visualisation and all kinds of insights and ideas will pop onto the page in front of you.

By the time you stand up, ready to take the first step that you see, you will be happy, eager and enthusiastic about getting on with achieving your goals.

A Positive Mental Attitude is indispensable to your success. You can be as positive as you want to be if you will simply take actions consistent with achieving your goals rather than actions that cause you to feel the negative emotions of worry, doubt, anger and fear.

If you do what other successful people do, if you use your mind to think, to exert mental control over the situation, you will be positive and cheerful most of the time. And you will reap the benefits enjoyed by all successful people.

CHOOSING SUCCESS

When is the last time you saw a rainforest with a clock in it? Seen a dog check his watch lately? Lions, giraffes and porcupines don't really seem to have much use for knowing when it's 5 o'clock.

But truth is, time is real in another sense. The planet we inhabit turns around every 24 hours. And tracking this gives us benchmarks. Points of reference we can track our progress against for the goals we have set.

And when we do an honest evaluation of our progress, we can determine to make it better; to challenge ourselves to live with more passion, love and adventure. To promise ourselves that if this next year is our last one, we will have done something with it. Congratulations on being part of the team that has made that commitment. There is another team you know. The other side...

And that team is a whole lot bigger than ours. Because that team is comprised of the "herd" that is satisfied with getting by, reacting to events and thinking they are the victim of outside circumstances.

What I've discovered about success and prosperity is that it has almost nothing to do with opportunities, chance, luck- or even training, education or skill. It has everything to do with consciousness, beliefs and even subconscious programming that you aren't aware of.

To paraphrase Reverend Eric Butterworth–poverty is not an absence of money and things–it is a state of mind. Prosperity is more than an abundance of money and things–it is also a state of mind.

Last year I was watching an interview with a baseball player, shortly after play resumed, following the September 11th attacks.

The announcer in his best somber announcer voiced intoned, "And I know this was tough on you because of your connections with New York. What was that like for you?"

He replied, "You know my uncle worked in that building for over 20 years. And I have many friends who live in Manhattan... blah, blah." He gets to the end and finally reveals that. his uncle retired a few years ago, was nowhere near the trade centre and all of his friends were fine.

It came to me then that what I was witnessing was the ballplayer trying to "own" being a victim. Like most of us, he was horrified and sickened by the tragedy.

And there is no doubt in my mind that anyone who saw those images on TV was victimised by them. They scarred the soul of all who saw them. But the more you let yourself "own" being a victim, the more events will harm your psyche.

A car driver goes out of control and drives through the window of a dry cleaner. You say, "If that would have happened two days ago, I was standing right there." That's you, trying to be a victim.

It's very easy to become a constant victim in a lot of areas of your life. I see it all the time in my softball league.

A guy twists his knee on a play. Next week he shows up with a brace on it. And the next. And the next and the next. It turns from a twisted knee to his "bad knee". He'll wear that brace for as long as he plays, because he owns the bad knee. Now he no longer has a bad knee, the bad knee has him.

You see this sometimes with sickly people. They may be raised in a family that doesn't express love very openly. They learn–on a subconscious level–that when they are sick, they get extra attention.

This starts a cycle that can last a lifetime. Even after they are grown up and married, they have programmed themselves to be sick. They catch every cold, every flu bug that goes around and every possible ailment.

They take a sweater everywhere because they "get a chill easily". They have a box of Kleenex on every table and nightstand in the house because they have "sinus problems". They spray the phone with disinfectant, wear a surgical mask on the bus and do nothing but think about being sick. So, of course, they are always sick.

Which begets the question, "Do they have seven boxes of Kleenex in the house because they have sinus problems–or do they have sinus problems because they have seven Kleenex in the house?"

Just like you get more attention when you are sick–you can get more attention when you get fired, wreck your car, get abused by your spouse and a host of other dramas.

On a subconscious level, you can manifest bad things happening to yourself. Even horrible things that you wouldn't wish on your worst enemy—you could be subconsciously be manifesting on yourself. It's hard to believe, but it can true.

I spent thirty-plus years being sick, allergic to air-conditioners, sodas and just about every food you can imagine.

I had to grill every waiter for the ingredient list of everything, buy special foods order special meals and just generally live like a prisoner. Once I got over being a victim, I got healthier and about 9/10^{ths} of my allergies disappeared.

Once I didn't want to be a victim anymore, all kind of others things changed as well. If you make that decision– things will change for you.

If you think you may still be falling prey to this syndrome, here's some things you can do to end it. When you see car crashes, bad situations and other tragedies, don't talk about how that could have been you. Don't ever affirm negative things like, "I've got a bad back," "I get sick easily," "My eyesight is bad," "I have problems with that," and other similar expressions.

Now you may be saying, "But it's true, I do have problems with XYZ!" Well of course you do. Because you keep affirming that. Which is programming your subconscious mind. Never "own" a negative trait or condition. You can affirm that you've had it in the past, but affirm also that those problems are over. What you can say is, "In the past, I have had problems with..."

When you are around "victim" people who are discussing all their problems, politely change the subject. If they persist (and many will), state that you really don't want to talk about negative things and suggest a better conversation. If they accuse you of being uncaring and demand to continue their commiserating (and some will) – get up and leave. And don't be bashful about it. We're talking about YOUR consciousness here – which is the most important thing you have in your life!

Evaluate every TV programme and movie you watch. Each book and story you read. Does the plot involve the underdog winning over the evil rich guy? Does the poor hero get the girl who leaves the millionaire? Is it the little guy fighting the big evil corporation?

You get the idea. Plots like these are designed to appeal to the herd's lack and limitation programming. They insidiously programme you that money and success are bad, rich people are evil and it's spiritual to be poor.

INCREDIBLE POWER OF FOCUS

One of the more important points I have made in writing about the "Nine Principles for Happiness and Healing" has been the idea that you really do create your own life and your own reality.

I know this idea has become a kind of personal growth cliche that many of us have heard over and over.

Many people, after continuing to experience the same old ups and downs and personal dramas over many years, get to the point where they dismiss this idea as charming but useless–or just plain wrong.

"If I'm creating this, then I'm certainly not doing it on purpose," they say. "It sure seems like this is happening to me, rather than that I'm creating it."

They just assume that it's all because "this and this and this and this are going on for me and I have no control over it and anyone who thinks I'm creating this doesn't understand what I'm going through."

Essentially, they are resigning themselves to be a victim of their circumstances.

We live in a universe of infinite complexity and many forces–way too many to keep track of–operate on us. Yes, it is true that we are not in control of everything that happens, because we are not in control of most of those infinite other parts of the universe.

In fact, the only thing you have total and complete control over is...

....Your Own Mind.

That is, if you learn how to exercise it.

Luckily, this one thing–your mind–that you do have control over gives you tremendous power.

By exercising control over your mind, you can get the rest of those infinite other parts of the universe to begin to march in formation.

The person who says, "If I'm creating this, it certainly isn't on purpose," is right. They are not creating what is happening to them "on purpose."

Who would purposely create failure or bad relationships or any other suffering? As I said in Principle #6, you can only do something that is not good for you, that is harmful to you, if you do it unconsciously. This means if you are creating something you don't want, you must be doing so unconsciously.

Your mind is running on automatic pilot, based on "software" (unconscious programming) installed when you were too young to know any better, by parents, teachers, friends, the media and other experiences and influences.

The key is to become more conscious, more aware... to get yourself off automatic pilot. Once you do this, you stop creating all the dramas and other garbage you don't want in your life.

How do you do this? One way, of course, is to use the Centre point programme, because listening to Holosync increases your ability to be consciously aware.

As you continue with the programme, doing this becomes easier and more automatic. That "watcher" part of you becomes stronger and stronger, until it is watching over everything and with that degree of conscious awareness, it is pretty difficult to create anything that is not beneficial for you.

You can help things along, however, by remembering and using a very important piece of wisdom. It's the fact that whatever you focus on manifests as reality in your life.

You are always focusing on something, whether you are aware of it or not. If I spent some time with you and heard your history, I could tell you what you are focusing on. How? By looking at the results you are getting in your life.

The results you get are always the result of your focus.

The problem is, this focus is usually not conscious focus, it's automatic focus. We unconsciously focus on something we don't want and then when we get it we feel like a victim and don't even stop to think that we created it in the first place.

And what is more, we don't realise we could choose to create something completely different if we could only get out of the cycle of unconsciously focusing on something other than what we want.

If you have a significant negative emotional experience (say, for instance, a relationship in which you are abused or mistreated in some way), a part of you is going to say: "Okay, I get it. There are people out there who can and will hurt me. Relationships can be dangerous and painful. I have to watch out for these people [or sometimes, relationships in general] and avoid them."

Unfortunately, to watch out for them and avoid them, you have to focus your mind on "people who could hurt me," or "bad relationships," and that focus draws more of what you don't want to you... and... actually makes these things you don't want (at least initially) attractive to you, so when they appear in your life you are drawn to them.

This is why many people keep having one relationship after another with the same person, but in different bodies.

This, of course, applies to everything, not just relationships. I'm just using relationships as an example.

Focusing on what you do not want, ironically, makes it happen.

Focusing on not being poor makes you poor.

Focusing on not making mistakes causes you to make mistakes.

Focusing on not having a bad relationship creates bad relationships.

Focusing on not being depressed makes you depressed.

Focusing on not smoking makes you want to smoke.

And so on. I think you get the idea.

The truth is, your mind cannot tell the difference between something you think about or focus on that you do want and something you think about or focus on but do not want.

The mind is a goal-seeking mechanism and an extremely effective one at that. Already, all the time, it is elegantly and precisely creating exactly what you focus on.

You are already a World Champion Expert at creating whatever you focus on. You couldn't get any better at it and you don't need to get any better at it.

When you focus on anything, your mind says: "Okay, we can do that" and starts figuring out how to do it. It doesn't ask whether you're focusing on it because you want it or because you do not want it.

It always assumes you want what you focus on and then it goes and makes it happen.

The more frequent and the more intense the focus, the faster and more completely you will create what you have focused on, which is why intense negative experiences create intense focus on what you do not want and tend to make you recreate what you don't want, over and over.

Most of the time, for most people, all the focusing and thinking is going by at warp speed, on automatic, without much, if any, conscious intention.

Your job is to learn how to direct this power by consciously directing your focus to the outcomes you want.

Once you do, everything changes. This does, however, take some work, because at first you have to swim upstream against the current of your old, unconscious habits and the current can be swift and strong.

First, you have to discover all the things you focus on that you do not want and I'm willing to bet there are quite a few ways more than you think. To the degree you're getting what you don't want, you are focusing, albeit unconsciously, on what you don't want.

Spend some time over the next few weeks, then, making a list of all the things you do not want as you notice yourself thinking about them.

Second, you have to get very clear about what you do want. Then, you have to examine each of the things you want and be sure they are not just something you do not want in disguise.

For instance, saying "I want a relationship where I am treated well" would not even be an issue if you had not had relationships where you were not treated well and even in making this seemingly positive statement you are focusing on not wanting to be mistreated.

Saying "I want a reliable car" wouldn't even come up if you weren't focusing on the fact that you don't want a car that breaks down and needs a lot of repairs.

After you've sorted out the things you habitually focus on that you do not want and know what you do want, you have to begin to notice each time you think about an outcome you do not want and consciously change your thinking, right in that moment, so you are instead focusing on what you do want.

Remember, you do not have to avoid things to be happy and get what you want. The urge to avoid something is a result of having had a negative emotional experience regarding that thing and trying to avoid things requires you to focus on them, which tells your brain to create them.

Not Good: You will be surprised how often you are thinking about what you do not want, how difficult it is to catch yourself doing it every time and–most of all–how difficult it is to switch your thinking to what you do want.

There is a strong momentum to keep thinking about that thing you want to avoid. As I said, the current is strong and swift, especially at first.

The solution? Practice, practice, practice. Persistence, persistence, persistence.

It's a very good idea to write down what you want, very specifically, so that your Fairy Godmother, were she to read it, would know exactly what to give you without any additional explanation.

Then, read what you have written to yourself, preferably out loud, several times a day, while seeing yourself, in your mind, already having what you want. The more emotion you can bring to it, the better.

Then, take whatever action is available to begin moving toward what you want. A good time to do this reading and visualising is when you first wake up and right before you go to bed.

I know this is work. Do it anyway. There is a price for everything and this is the price you must pay to get what you want. Be prepared to pay it. It will be worth it, I promise. And be prepared to pay for a while before you get results. Stick with it.

Another way to change your focus is to ask questions. As an example, I'll ask you one right now. What did you have for breakfast this morning?

To answer this question (even to just internally process the question), you had to shift your focus from whatever your mind was focussed on (hopefully) to today's breakfast.

This means that to change your focus, all you have to do is... ask yourself a question! It also means you better be careful what questions you ask yourself.

Good questions include: "How can I get X?" "How can I do X?" "How can I be X?" By asking these kinds of questions, you get your mind to focus on what you want to have, do or be.

Then, your mind takes over and answers the question... solves the problem... and creates what you want. You just have to provide the focus, take whatever action presents itself and be persistent (some things take time).

I would do away with questions like: "What's wrong with me?" or "Why can't I find someone to love me?" and so on. Your mind will find an answer to any question you give it, including these disempowering questions.

Learn to say "How can I...?" when you don't know what to do, instead of "I can't," and (if you are persistent in asking) the universe will send you the answer, every time. Learn to be conscious in what you focus on and your whole life will change.

This all may seem very utopian to you or overly simplistic or like a lot of work. I assure you it is not utopian (it's the way all successful people think), it is simple, but not simplistic and yes, it is work, at first.

The great Napoleon Hill, who spent over 60 years studying the most effective and most successful people of the 20th century, concluded that–without exception, mind you–"whatever the mind can conceive and believe, it can achieve."

He at first suspected there had to be exceptions, but toward the end of his life he said he had to admit he had not found any.

Go over that again: "Whatever the mind can conceive and believe, it can achieve."

It will take some time to learn how to consciously focus your mind. It will require some effort. You will fail many times and it will seem difficult.

But at a certain point you will "get it" and at that point it will become as automatic as the unconscious focusing you have been doing. When that happens, a whole new universe of power will open to you.

SUCCESS THROUGH GOAL-SETTING

The ability to set goals and make plans for their accomplishment is the "master skill" of success. It is the single-most important skill that you can learn and perfect.

Goal-setting will do more to help you achieve the things you want in life than will anything else you've been exposed to. Becoming an expert at goal-setting and goal-achieving is something that you absolutely must do if you wish to fulfil your potential as a human being.

Goals enable you to do the work you want to do, to live where you want to live, to be with the people you enjoy and to become the kind of person you want to become.

And there is no limit to the financial rewards you can obtain. All you have to do is to set a goal for financial success, make a plan and then work the plan until you succeed in that area.

The payoff for setting goals and making plans is being able to choose the kind of life you want to live.

So why do so few people set goals? According to the best research, less than 3 percent of Americans have written goals and less than 1 per cent review and rewrite their goals on a daily basis.

So the reasons why people don't set goals have been of considerable interest to me. I think that there are five basic reasons why people don't set goals.

The first reason is that they are simply not serious. Whenever I speak with a man or woman who has achieved something remarkable, I learn that the achievement occurred after that person decided to "get serious."

Until you become completely serious and totally determined about your goals, nothing really happens.

The second reason why people don't set goals is that they don't understand the importance of goals.

We find that young men and women who begin setting goals very early in life invariably come from families in which the importance of goals is emphasised. The discussion that takes place around your family dinner table is one of the most powerful formative influences in your life.

If your parents didn't have goals, didn't talk about goals, didn't encourage you to set goals and didn't talk about people outside the family circle who had goals and were moving toward a higher level of achievement, then you very likely grew up with the idea that goals are not even a part of normal existence. This is the case for most people. And for many years, it was the case for me.

The third reason why people don't set goals is because they don't know how to do it. One of the greatest tragedies of our educational system is that you can receive 15 to 18 years of education in our schools and never once receive a single hour of instruction on how to set goals.

Yet we find that in certain schools where goal-setting programmes have been introduced since first grade, young people become excited about goal-setting–even if the goal is only to increase the scores by 5 or 10 per cent over the course of the semester or to be on time every day in the course of a month. Children become so excited about achieving goals that by the third or fourth grade, they love to go to school. They get the best grades. They are seldom absent. They are excited about themselves and about their lives.

So encourage your children to set worthwhile and realistic goals from an early age.

The fourth reason why people don't set goals is fear of rejection. The fear of rejection is caused by destructive criticism in early childhood and is manifested, in adulthood, in the fear of criticism by others.

Many people hold back from setting worthwhile goals because they have found that every time they do set a goal, somebody steps up and tells them that they can't achieve it or that they will lose their money or waste their time.

Because each of us is strongly influenced by the opinions of those around us, one of the first things that you must learn when you begin setting goals is to keep your goals confidential. Don't tell anyone about them.

Often, it's the fear of criticism that, more than any other single factor, stops you from goal-setting in the first place. So keep your goals to yourself, with one exception. Share your goals only with others who are committed to achieving goals of their own and who really want you to be successful and achieve your goals as well.

Other than that, don't tell anybody about your goals, so no one is in a position to criticise you or to discourage you from setting your goals.

The fifth reason why people don't set goals–and perhaps the most important reason of all–is the fear of failure. People don't set goals because they are afraid that they might fail.

In fact, the fear of failure is probably the greatest single obstacle to success in adult life. It can hold you back more than any other psychological problem.

The primary reason why you fear failure is simply this: You probably do not understand the role that failure plays in achievement. The fact is that it is impossible to succeed without failing. Failure is an indispensable prerequisite for success.

GREAT SUCCESS PRECEDED BY GREAT FAILURE

If you wish to fulfil your potential, you have to be willing to risk failure over and over and over, because there is no way that you can ever accomplish worthwhile goals until you have fallen on your face so many times that you have eventually learned the lessons that you need for great achievement.

In doing research for his classic book The Law of Success, Napoleon Hill interviewed more than 500 of the most successful men and women in America.

All of them admitted to him that they had achieved their greatest successes just one step beyond the point where they had experienced their greatest failures.

A key to succeeding through goal-setting is expecting temporary setbacks and obstacles as inevitable parts of the goal-achieving process.

Now, in order to be successful, you need to focus your mental and physical energy in a single direction towards a pre-determined objective. People who are especially energetic or talented have a hard time with this. They are the ones who try to do several things at once and end up doing nothing well.

Setting well-defined goals enables you to channel your efforts and focus your energy toward something that's important to you.

Goal-setting gives you a target to aim at and enables you to develop the self-discipline to continue working towards your target rather than becoming distracted and going off in other directions.

Let me share with you five keys that will help you to reach your goals more effectively. Each of these keys starts with one of the letters in the 'word' goals.

Whenever you find yourself getting off the track, simply repeat the word goals and think about how each letter stands for a key that just might apply to your current situation. The first letter is G and it stands for get to it.

Sometimes, the only difference between a successful person and a failure is that the successful person has the courage to get started, to do something, to begin moving towards the accomplishment of a specific goal.

For example, when I was younger, I realised that because of my limited education, I was stuck in a low-paying job. I began reading the want ads and decided that I wanted to work in advertising, especially as a copywriter.

I went to an advertising agency and applied for the job of writing advertisements. The head of the agency was very polite, but he told me that I was unskilled and totally unsuited for the position. He thanked me for coming in and wished me luck.

Now I was back on the street, but I had a goal. I wanted to be an advertising copywriter. I immediately took the first step, which was to learn more about how to write copy, so that I would not be turned down in the future because of a lack of ability.

I went to the local library and checked out books on the subject of advertising and copywriting. Over the next 12 months, I checked out and read every single book in the library on the subject.

Meanwhile, I read magazines and newspapers and thought about how I could improve their advertising. I wrote sample advertisements and began taking them to advertising agencies.

To make a long story short, at the end of the 12 months, two of the largest advertising agencies in the country offered me a job as a copywriter and I accepted one of those offers. My income doubled.

I had worked at other jobs in the meantime. But I had never lost sight of my goal and I had kept on doing the things that I needed to do to put myself in a position to eventually achieve my goal.

You, too, may have a long-range goal. In order to achieve it, you need to sit down and make a list of all the steps that you will have to take to get from where you are to where you want to be. Then begin with the first and most obvious thing that you can do on that list.

Complete it and then start on number two. Don't worry about the long term. Just concentrate on the obvious first step that you can take. Surprisingly enough, everything else will take care of itself.

The Confucian saying, "A journey of a thousand leagues begins with a single step," is so popular in so many languages because it is so true.

The second letter, O, stands for opportunity. Successful people do not wait for opportunities to turn their goals into reality; rather, they make their opportunities, because they are perfectly clear about the kind of life they wish to create.

Once you have taken the time to decide exactly what you want, you will experience an endless flow of opportunities that will help move you in that direction.

For example, a young woman worked for me as an executive secretary. At the same time, she had a goal to be a successful real-estate agent and investor. So while she worked for me, she regularly took night courses to get her real-estate-agent's license and also to learn how to buy and sell real estate profitably.

Over the course of an year, she and her husband bought, fixed up and sold three houses. They made more money from their real-estate transactions than they did from their jobs. At the end of the year, she passed the test and got her real-estate-agent's license.

Within a few days of getting her license, she and her husband were sitting in a small restaurant and they got into a conversation with a woman at the next table.

It turned out that this woman was a very successful real-estate agent who needed an executive assistant to work with her and learn the real-estate profession.

They got along so well that my executive secretary was offered the job, where she would be earning double what she could earn as a secretary and have an unlimited upside potential.

My secretary did not wait for an opportunity to come to her. She set a goal, made a plan and went to work to prepare herself for the opportunity when it arose.

The letter A stands for ability. Many people hesitate to set high, challenging goals because they lack the ability necessary to turn those goals into reality. But remember that we all lacked knowledge and experience when we started out in our careers or fields of expertise.

Do you remember when you started your first job? You probably felt a little clumsy, inadequate and unsure about how to do it well. As you progressed and got more experience, you became more and more confident and in many cases, you did an excellent job without even thinking much about it.

Since you gain the ability necessary for high achievement through knowledge and experience, if you increase the speed at which you acquire both of those, you increase the speed at which you move ahead.

The letter L stands for leadership. Leadership is simply the ability to get results. And you begin to get results when you accept full responsibility for yourself, for your job and for the outputs required in your position.

You demonstrate leadership when you refuse to make excuses or blame anyone or anything for the problems you are having. The acceptance of the responsibility of leadership enables you to move ahead and take action.

When you are not satisfied with your job or income and you sit down and make a written plan to change it and then take action on that plan, without waiting for anyone's approval or permission, you are behaving like a leader.

The final letter, S, stands for stay with it—the resolution to persist in the face of adversity until you succeed. Between you and every goal that you wish to achieve, there is a series of obstacles and the bigger the goal, the bigger the obstacles.

Your decision to be, have and do something out of the ordinary entails facing difficulties and challenges that are out of the ordinary as well. Sometimes your greatest asset is simply your ability to stay with it longer than anyone else.

When you look around you, you will see that all achievement is the triumph of persistence. You will see men and women everywhere who are struggling with and overcoming adversities in order to accomplish something that is important to them. And so can you.

So these are the words and phrases to remember in setting and achieving goals:

The first is get to it! Get started; take the first action at hand.

The second is opportunity. Begin to prepare yourself now so that you will be ready for the opportunities that will inevitably arise. The third is ability. Resolve to learn what you need to know to live the kind of life you want to live.

The fourth word is leadership. Take charge of your time and your life and accept responsibility for your results.

And, finally, stay with it. If you stay with it long enough, nothing can stop you from finally winning through.

ACHIEVING DREAMS

While most people spend most of their lives struggling to earn a living, a much smaller number seem to have everything going their way.

Instead of just earning a living, the smaller group is busily working at building and enjoying a fortune. Everything just seems to work out for them. And here sits the much larger group, wondering how life can be so unfair, so complicated and unjust.

What's the major difference between the little group with so much and the larger group with so little?

Despite all of the factors that affect our lives–like the kind of parents we have, the schools we attended, the part of the country we grew up in–none has as much potential power for affecting our futures as our ability to dream.

Dreams are a projection of the kind of life you want to lead. Dreams can drive you. Dreams can make you skip over obstacles. When you allow your dreams to pull you, they unleash a creative force that can overpower any obstacle in your path.

To unleash this power, though, your dreams must be well defined. A fuzzy future has little pulling power. Well-defined dreams are not fuzzy. Wishes are fuzzy. To really achieve your dreams, to really have your future plans pull you forward, your dreams must be vivid.

If you've ever hiked a fourteen thousand-foot peak in the Rocky Mountains, one thought has surely come to mind "How did the settlers of this country do it?"

How did they get from the East Coast to the West Coast? Carrying one day's supply of food and water is hard enough. Can you imagine hauling all of your worldly goods with you... mile after mile, day after day, month after month?

These people had big dreams. They had ambition. They didn't focus on the hardship of getting up the mountain.

In their minds, they were already on the other side—their bodies just hadn't got them there yet!

Despite all of their pains and struggles, all of the births and deaths along the way, those who made it to the other side had a single vision: To reach the land of continuous sunshine and extraordinary wealth. To start over where anything and everything was possible.

Their dreams were stronger than the obstacles in their way.

You've got to be a dreamer. You've got to envision the future. You've got to see California while you're climbing fourteen thousand-foot peaks. You've got to see the finish line while you're running the race. You've got to hear the cheers when you're in the middle of a monster project.

And you've got to be willing to put yourself through the paces of doing the uncomfortable until it becomes comfortable. Because that's how you realise your dreams.

MANAGING TIME

Perhaps the greatest single problem that people have today is "time poverty." Working people have too much to do and too little time for their personal lives.

Most people feel overwhelmed with responsibilities and activities and the harder they work, the further behind they feel. This sense of being on a never-ending treadmill can cause you to fall into the reactive/responsive mode of living.

Instead of clearly deciding what you want to do, you continually react to what is happening around you. Pretty soon you lose all sense of control. You feel that your life is running you, rather than you running your life.

On a regular basis, you have to stand back and take stock of yourself and what you're doing. You have to stop the clock and do some serious thinking about who you are and where you are going.

You have to evaluate your activities in the light of what is really important to you. You must master your time rather than becoming a slave to the constant flow of events and demands on your time. And you must organise your life to achieve balance, harmony and inner peace.

Taking action without thinking is the cause of every failure. Your ability to think is the most valuable trait that you possess. If you improve the quality of your thinking, you improve the quality of your life, sometimes immediately.

Time is your most precious resource. It is the most valuable thing you have. It is perishable, it is irreplaceable and it can not be saved. It can only be reallocated from activities of lower value to activities of higher value.

All work requires time. And time is absolutely essential for the important relationships in your life. The very act of taking a moment to think about your time before you spend it will begin to improve your personal time management immediately.

I used to think that time management was only a business tool, like a calculator or a cellular telephone. It was something that you used so that you could get more done in a shorter period of time and eventually be paid more money.

Then I learned that time management is not a peripheral activity or skill. It is the core skill upon which everything else in life depends.

In your work or business life, there are so many demands on your time from other people that very little of your time is yours to use as you choose.

However, at home and in your personal life you can exert a tremendous amount of control over how you use your time. And it is in this area that I want to focus.

Personal time management begins with you. It begins with your thinking through what is really important to you in life. And it only makes sense if you organise it around specific things that you want to accomplish.

You need to set goals in three major areas of your life.

First, you need family and personal goals. These are the reasons why you get up in the morning, why you work hard and upgrade your skills, why you worry about money and sometimes feel frustrated by the demands on your time.

What are your personal and family goals, both tangible and intangible?

A tangible family goal could be a bigger house, a better car, a larger television set, a vacation or anything else that costs money.

An intangible goal would be to build a higher quality relationship with your spouse and children, to spend more time with your family going for walks or reading books. Achieving these family and personal goals are the real essence of time management and its major purpose.

The second area of goals are your business and career goals. These are the "how" goals, the means by which you achieve your personal, "why" goals.

How can you achieve the level of income that will enable you to fulfil your family goals? How can you develop the skills and abilities to stay ahead of the curve in your career?

Business and career goals are absolutely essential, especially when balanced with family and personal goals.

The third type of goals are your personal development goals. Remember, you can't achieve much more on the outside than what you have achieved on the inside. Your outer life will be a reflection of your inner life.

If you wish to achieve worthwhile things in your personal and your career life, you must become a worthwhile person in your own self-development. You must build yourself if you want to build your life.

Perhaps the greatest secret of success is that you can become anything you really want to become to achieve any goal that you really want to achieve. But in order to do it, you must go to work on yourself and never stop.

Once you have a list of your personal and family goals, your business and career goals and your self-development goals, you can then organise the list by priority. This brings us to the difference between priorities and posteriorties.

In order to get your personal time under control, you must decide very clearly upon your priorities. You must decide on the most important things that you could possible be doing to give yourself the same amount of happiness, satisfaction and joy in life.

But at the same time, you must establish posteriorties as well. Just as priorities are things that you do more of and sooner, posteriorties are things that you do less of and later.

The fact is, your calendar is full. You have no spare time. Your time is extremely valuable. Therefore, for you to do anything new, you will have to stop doing something old.

In order to get into something, you will have to get out of something else. In order to pick something up, you will have to put something down.

Before you make any new commitment of your time, you must firmly decide what activities you are going to discontinue in your personal life. If you want to spend more time with your family, *for example*, you must decide what activities you currently engage in that are preventing you from doing so.

A principle of time management says that hard time pushes out soft time. This means that hard time, such as working, will push out soft time, such as the time you spend with your family. If you don't get your work done at the office because you don't use your time well, you almost invariably have to rob that time from your family.

As a result, because your family is important to you, you find yourself in a values conflict. You feel stressed and irritable. You feel a tremendous amount of pressure.

You know in your heart that you should be spending more time with the important people in your life, but because you didn't get your work done, you have to fulfil those responsibilities before you can spend time with your spouse and children.

Think of it this way. Every minute you waste during the waking day is time that your family will ultimately be deprived of. So concentrate on working when you are at work so that you can concentrate on your family when you are at home.

There are three key questions that you can ask yourself continually to keep your personal life in balance.

The first question is, "What is really important to me?" Whenever you find yourself with too much to do and too little time, stop and ask yourself, "What is it that is really important for me to do in this situation?" Then, make sure that what you are doing is the answer to that question.

The second question is, "What are my highest value activities?" In your personal life, this means, "What are the things that I do that give me the greatest pleasure and satisfaction? Of all the things that I could be doing at any one time, what are the things that I could do to add the greatest value to my life?"

And the final question for you to ask over and over again is, "What is the most valuable use of my time right now?" Since you can only do one thing at a time, you must constantly organise your life so that you are doing one thing, the most important thing, at every moment.

Personal time management enables you to choose what to do first, what to do second and what not to do at all. It enables you to organise every aspect of your life so that you can get the greatest joy, happiness and satisfaction out of everything you do.

PROJECT MANAGEMENT

Some skills are peripheral to success. It's nice to have them, but they don't make much of a difference one way or another.

There are other skills, however, that are absolutely essential to your fulfilling your potential and you must develop them to a fairly high degree if you are to achieve all of your goals.

One of these absolutely essential skills is the ability to manage projects of various sizes. A project is defined as a multi task job, the kind that you engage in every day in the process of making a living and carrying on the business of your life.

To be a success, you must be good at project management.

One of the great dangers in project management is feeling that we already know all we need to know about the subject.

Too many people take their ability to do several jobs at once or in a row, for granted. They fall into the intelligence trap of the low performer. They use their intelligence to point out to themselves and to others how confident and capable they already are. They join the ranks of the "unconscious incompetent."

The unconscious incompetent is the person who does not know and he does not know that he does not know. Project management is a function not just of those who build hydroelectric dams or construct huge skyscrapers.

You organise and engage in a project each time you go shopping at the grocery store. If you are in sales, every prospect you are working on developing into a regular customer is a project. If you are going out for the evening with another person, you are planning and organising a project.

And here is a key point. Your ability to organise and carry through a project successfully is a key skill for success. It is the essential art of management. It is the way that you multiply yourself and your results.

Your ability to manage projects of all kinds is absolutely indispensable to your achieving financial independence and moving to the top in your field.

Many people can type, but few people can type 80 or 90 words a minute without mistakes. Lakhs of people know how to operate computers, but only a few can use the computer so skilfully as to maximise its capacities in helping them to do their work and accomplish their objectives.

Many people can sell, but the top 10 percent of sales-people still open 80 per cent of the new accounts and make most of the money. Project management is similar. Everyone knows how to carry out a multi-task job. But few people are good at it. Most are partially organised and partially disorganised.

They spend too much time, too much money and they make too many mistakes in getting from Point A to Point B. They don't manage the projects in their lives skilfully because they don't know how critical this ability is to accomplishing virtually everything else they could possibly want in life.

To succeed in life, you need leverage; you need assistance. If you want to achieve big things and live a great life, you need the help of lots of people.

You need to be very good at coordinating the activities of several people in a single direction toward a pre-determined objective. If you don't develop your skills at project management, you will still be involved in projects, but you will always be a team member and never be a team leader.

The economic strength of America is due to many things and one of the most important is specialisation of tasks or division of labour. This simply means that most people, instead of trying to be jacks-of-all-trades, specialise and become very good at doing one or two things.

Today, one of the most popular words in business is outsourcing. This means that, instead of hiring or building a capability in-house, you delegate an entire function of your company to another company that specialises in doing only that one task.

Many people are finding that it is cheaper to have functions such as payroll, accounting, drop-shipping, manufacturing, assembly, delivery and distribution, plus a thousand other tasks, done by other companies that specialise in those areas than it is to do them in-house. Your whole life is a process of outsourcing.

Whether you are aware of it or not, you are continually outsourcing tasks and activities to a hundred other enterprises, such as grocery stores, restaurants, dry cleaners, quick-oil-change franchises and tailors.You don't bother to learn how to do those things yourself. It is much faster and cheaper for you to turn the tasks over to people who specialise in them. They can do the tasks faster, better and with fewer mistakes than you ever could imagine.

By outsourcing, you free up your time to do more and more of the things that you do best and for which you are the highest paid. It is one of the keys to developing the leverage that turns you into a multiplication sign with your talents and abilities.

In project management, you engage in a systematic and well-organised process of outsourcing the various tasks that need to be done to achieve a particular objective. You develop synergy by pulling together the talents and abilities of a lot of people toward the accomplishment of a single goal.

By working together as a team, a group of people with different talents can accomplish extraordinary things. And your ability to get all members of a team pulling in the same direction is the key to your maximising yourself in your life and in your career. To unleash the cooperative capabilities of a team of people toward the achievement of a multi-task job, the operative word should be harmony. One of the most important things you can do is to strive for harmony among the people working with you and for you.

Project management is an art. It requires thought. Whenever you have a large job to do, your very first step is to sit down with a pad of paper and begin to "think on paper."

All highly successful men and women think on paper. They write things down before they begin. They make lists and they make sub-lists.

They use calculators. And they analyse every detail of a large project before they begin. They think it through from beginning to end.

And in so doing, they save enormous amounts of time and money and they seem to get more done in a few months than the average person gets done in years.

Project management takes practise, as does anything else. It requires self-discipline. It requires the willpower to hold yourself back from plunging into a task before thinking it through in advance.

Many people are in a "reactive-responsive" mode. They react to whatever is happening around them and they respond to however they feel at the moment. They leap into things and then they leap out.

They rush to make judgments, come to decisions and take actions without bothering to analyse the situation thoroughly. They make enormous numbers of mistakes and are seen by others as incompetent and disorganised. Don't be one of those people.

When you decide to become excellent at project management, you begin to apply a systematic process such as the one I will describe. Your ability to achieve multi-task jobs is to control everything else you accomplish. And it's not that difficult to learn.

In any project, the first thing to do is start at the goal and work back. Stephen Covey says, "Begin with the end in mind." Dr. Roberto Assagioli suggests that you begin all activities by creating the ideal result or outcome that you desire, either on paper or in your mind, before you proceed to planning and organising.

Robert Fritz, in his book The Path of Least Resistance, says that the most powerful of all organising principles is a future vision of a clear goal to which you and others, are committed.

In his research on peak performers, Dr. Charles Garfield found that a person's ability to project his mind forward to the desired end state, to the goal as if it were already achieved, the task as though it were completed perfectly in every respect, is the starting point of maximum achievement.

In any case, every project begins with your clearly defining exactly what you want to accomplish and what it will look like if it is accomplished perfectly.

For example, let's say that you decide to take a two-week trip to the Caribbean next winter. This is a project.

You begin by defining what an ideal Caribbean vacation would consist of in every detail. You think about the hotel, the beaches, the daytime and evening activities you enjoy, the kind of people and service you want to experience and, of course, your budget.

With all of those ingredients and perhaps more, in mind, you come up with a clear description of the perfect winter holiday in the sun.

You then make a list of everything that you will have to do in order to achieve that final goal. You investigate the various Caribbean islands you could visit.

You call more than one travel agent, to find out if there are particular packages, including air fare and hotels, that you can purchase at excellent prices well in advance.

You plan your budget and determine where and when you will get the money that you require for this trip.

You consider your work responsibilities and think through how you will arrange being away for two weeks without your company or your clients suffering at the time.

If you have children, you think through their requirements, whether they will come with you or stay with someone while you are away.

If you have animals, you think about how they will be taken care of.

You think about the various clothes and accessories that you will need for a two-week Caribbean vacation.

Once you have determined exactly how you want the goal to look when it is complete, you set specific dates and deadlines, starting from the departure date back to the present.

By doing this, you have a clear time line from where you are to where you need to be on the day that the plane takes off.

The next step in project management is to organise your list of all the things that will need to be done for you to get to your goal, the completion of your project.

There are two ways to organise a list in project management.

The first way is sequential. This is when one step follows another. The first must be done before the second can be started.

The second must be completed before the third can be started and so on. These are often called dependent activities. One depends on the successful completion of another. This is a key point to remember in managing a project of any size.

The second type of activities in project management are parallel or concurrent activities. These are tasks that can be worked on at the same time, separate and apart from other activities.

For example, if you are planning a new brochure or newsletter, you could be writing the copy at the same time you are selecting paper stock or gathering possible photographs to illustrate the content.

Once you have the goal in mind and have listed everything that you must do to achieve the goal and organised everything in terms of whether it is sequential or concurrent, you are ready for the core exercise of effective project management.

It is the key to your future in the world of work. It is the process of selection and delegation.

The bigger the project, the more people, the more specialists in different fields, will be required to carry it through to successful completion.

Your ability to select the right people and then to delegate effectively to them will determine, as much as any other factor, your success or failure. A mistake in selection or a miscommunication in delegation can be enough to derail the entire project or to set it back or to have it run over budget.

Many men and women have been able to shoot ahead in their careers by taking on a project and then performing in an exemplary fashion.

Others have found themselves bypassed for promotion because when they were given a project to carry out, they did not take it seriously enough and their lack of results undermined the confidence of their superiors in their abilities.

Project management is serious stuff. Almost all problems in business are management problems and this means project-management problems.

This is often why a new manager comes in and replaces everyone on the team. He recognises that the reason why the job isn't getting done is probably because the person in charge of the multi-task job, manufacturing, sales, distribution or whatever, is not up to par.

When you build your team, you make a statement about your capability as a manager. As much as 95 percent of your success in the business world will be determined by your ability to select the right people to help you.

Most of your problems in business come from attempting to get the job done with difficult, incompetent people.

Your job is to select the very best people available to you who can do the job. Examine a person's track record carefully. Check references. Talk to other people about the task and get opinions concerning the individual's ability to do it in an excellent fashion.

Be careful about your choices and be adamant about assigning key tasks to the very best people. This will save you time and trouble. Once you have selected the individuals to carry out the specific parts of the project, you must delegate effectively to each of them.

Assign specific responsibilities for each task necessary to complete the project to specific individuals, each of whom has a deadline as well.

Tell each person what is to be done, when it is to be done, what standards of performance you require and what the overall project will look like when it is complete. Leave nothing to chance.

The more people know about the what and why of the total job, the more capable they are of carrying out their individual functions.

Lack of clarity is the single greatest contributor to failure in project management. For this reason, it is important that you meet regularly with the members of your team, either individually or together.

You keep in touch with them on a regular basis. You keep them informed. You give and receive, feedback. And the more important the project is, the more you stay on top of it.

Just as it is important for you to think on paper in organising a project for yourself, it is helpful for you to use a chalk-board or a flip chart when you are meeting with the members of your team.

The more visual you can make the project and the process of achieving the goal, the more likely it is that each task will be completed on schedule and to the standards you have set.

You supervise the project by measuring people's progress toward their individual deadlines. Your supervision of the project is what makes it all come together.

The rule is "Inspect what you expect." Never assume anything. Remember, Murphy's Laws were developed by men and women managing projects of various sizes.

You know some of these laws:

Anything that can go wrong will go wrong.

However much you budget it will cost more than you expect.

However long you allow it will take longer than you thought.

Of all the things that can go wrong, the worst possible thing will go wrong at the worst possible time.

And, of course, you've heard the corollary to Murphy's Laws:

Murphy was an optimist.

Finally, in project management there is always a critical event or limiting step. This is the one thing that absolutely, positively has to be done to a set standard for the project to be successful.

It is in this area that you must take personal responsibility and focus your personal attention on making sure that everything is done right. Keep your eyes on the ball, even if you delegate or outsource the task.

You can use project management to develop a new account, to increase your income, to attain a high level of physical health and fitness, to plan a vacation, to move across the country, to start and build a business, to write a book, paint a picture or sail a catamaran around the world.

In every case, the proper use of project-management techniques, such as those we have discussed here, can give you the winning edge. It can enable you to kick in the afterburners for your life and your career.

The skill of project management will enable you to move ahead further and faster than you ever could without it. Although the steps to project management are simple, the skill of project management is complex and it is vital to your success.

The cumulative results of your developing the skills of project management will enable you to accomplish bigger and bigger tasks with greater responsibilities and greater income, with greater rewards of all kinds. Project management is a powerful key to the future.

TRANSFORMING BAD HABITS

Your habits have been developed from early childhood as the result of things that you have chosen to do or not to do.

Your entire life is the result of your past choices and decisions.

And like all of us, you probably have some bad habits that have held, you back from your true potential.

But here's the good news: Since you are always free to choose, you can make new choices and decisions today that will determine what happens to you in the future.

One of your main objectives in life is to develop new habits and make them your masters, while at the same time overriding and setting aside old habits that may be interfering with your progress.

You have two major types of habits. You have habits that revolve around your desires and you have habits that revolve around your fears.

The habits that revolve around your desires for health, happiness, financial independence and success are life-enhancing. They are the habits that have brought you the success you enjoy today.

The habits that revolve around your fears, on the other hand, act as brakes on your potential. They hold you back. They interfere with your success. They trip you up on a regular basis. They cause you to sell yourself short and settle for far less than your potential.

Dr. Martin Seligman, in his book, Learned Optimism, wrote about the chief psychological phenomenon of modern life. He called it "learned helplessness."

Based on his 25 years of research, he discovered that virtually every person has one or more areas where they feel helpless and unable to do something that they really want to do.

Seligman's research demonstrated how animals can be trained to feel that they are helpless. In one example, he put a dog into a cage with a glass wall in the middle that separated the dog from a bowl of food.

The dog was hungry and tried to get at the food but kept banging his nose on the glass. After several hours, Seligman removed the glass. And what happened then? The dog, who was still hungry, sat only a few inches away from the food and never even attempted to eat it.

The dog had learned to feel helpless. The dog had become so convinced that he was incapable of getting to the food that even when the obstacles were removed, he just sat there with his stomach growling.

There are dozens of experiments like this. In every case, it is clear that animals and human beings for that matter, learn to feel helpless. They develop habits of thought that hold them back from reaching their full potential.

If someone were to tell you that you could learn to type 30, 40 or 50 words per minute by taking a typing course and practicing an hour each day for the next few months, you would shrug your shoulders and say, "Of course!"

Everybody knows that you can acquire a particular physical skill by learning how it is done and then repeating it over and over again until it becomes automatic.

But when it comes to mental habit patterns, most people are a little baffled. They don't realise that you can learn mental habit patterns by following exactly the same process that you would use to learn physical habit patterns.

And mental habit patterns will have a far greater impact on your life and happiness than any physical habit pattern ever could.

Once you have recognised the old, negative habit patterns that do not serve your purposes, you can determine what new habit patterns you would like to adopt. Begin this process by looking around and determining the people that you admire the most, both living and dead.

Ask yourself: What qualities do they have? Which of their characteristics do you most wish to have for yourself? Then make a plan to incorporate those ideal habits into your own character and personality.

You know that you can shape a piece of clay into any desired form. You can also shape your own character and personality by simply deciding to do so. I won't say that it is easy.

Changing your beliefs and attitudes about yourself is one of the most difficult undertakings you will ever face. But it is definitely possible and achievable if you dedicate the necessary time and effort.

How long does it take to develop a new habit pattern? It depends on how complex the habit pattern is. You can develop a simple habit pattern in 14 to 21 days.

For example, if you want to begin getting up half an hour earlier so that you can plan and organise your day, it might take just two to three weeks to develop the habit.

If you want to develop a new habit pattern of behaviour that does deeper into your character, it might take several months or even a year or more.

The most important point is that, no matter how long it takes, the end result is achievable if you are really determined.

The habits of success have been studied by the great thinkers and philosophers for at least 2,500 years. After personally studying the subject for more than 30 years, I have found that the very best people have the very best habits.

Based on these findings, I have identified seven habits that you need to develop if you want to perform at your very maximum in everything you do.

GOAL ORIENTATION

You need to become a habitual goal setter and dedicate yourself to working from clear, written goals every day of your life.

RESULT ORIENTATION

Result orientation is made up of two practises.

The first is the practise of continuously learning so that you become better at what you do.

The second practise is that of time management, which means setting very clear priorities on what you do and then concentrating single-mindedly on the most valuable use of your time.

ACTION ORIENTATION

This is really the most important habit for material success. It is the ability to get on with the job and get it done fast.

Fast tempo in whatever you do is essential to your success. You need to overcome procrastination, push aside your fears and launch 100% toward the achievement of your most important goals.

PEOPLE ORIENTATION

This is your decision to cultivate within yourself the habits of patience, kindness, compassion and understanding.

Virtually all of your happiness in life will come from your ability to get along well with other people. And getting along well with other people is based on a set of habits that you have learned or failed to learn, from childhood.

But it is never too late to become a wonderful human being in your relationships with other. The more you practise being a truly excellent person in your relationship with others, the more you will internalise those qualities and actually become that person.

HEALTH ORIENTATION

This means that you must make a conscious effort to eat the right foods in the right proportions. You must exercise on a regular basis, continually using every muscle and joint of your body to keep it young and fit.

And finally, you must have regular habits of rest and recreation that will enable you, in combination with diet and exercise, to live a long, full life.

Remember, your health is the single most important thing you have and it is completely dependent upon the habits you develop with regard to the way you live.

HONESTY AND INTEGRITY

In the final analysis, the character you develop as you go through life is more important than virtually anything else.

Honesty means that you practise the "reality principle" in everything you do. You are completely objective with yourself and with the world around you. You set very clear values for yourself and you organise your life around your values.

You develop a vision for yourself and then you live your life consistent with your highest ideals. You never compromise your integrity or peace of mind for anyone or anything. This attitude of honesty will enable you to enjoy all of the other success habits that you are developing.

SELF-DISCIPLINE

Your ability to discipline yourself, to master yourself, to control yourself, goes hand in hand with success in every area of life.

My favourite definition of self-discipline comes from Elbert Hubbard. He said, "Self-discipline is the ability to make yourself do what you should do, when you should do it, whether you feel like it or not."

Every one of these habits, goal orientation, result orientation, action orientation, people orientation, health orientation, honesty and self-discipline can be developed.

The following is a seven step method you can use to internalise any habit or group of habits that you want to make a permanent part of your character and personality.

1. Decide clearly on the new habit. Write it down as a goal in the form of a present tense, personal, positive affirmation.

For example, if you want to develop the habit of self-discipline, you write, "I am an extremely well-disciplined individual in everything I do."

2. Repeat your affirmation as often as possible and with as much enthusiasm and conviction as possible.

The more times you repeat this command, the more likely it is that your sub-conscious mind will ultimately accept it and begin to adjust your thoughts, words and behaviours to be consistent with it.

3. Visualise yourself as if you already had the new habit pattern. Imagine yourself as already being exactly the person that you want to become in the future.

Remember, your subconscious mind is activated and programmed by mental pictures. All improvement in your life and character begin with an improvement in your mental pictures. Use visualisation on a regular basis in conjunction with your positive affirmations.

4. Emotionalise the affirmation and the visualisation. Take a few minutes each day to actually experience the feeling of being the excellent, outstanding human being that you have decided to become.
5. Launch into your new habit with conviction. Assume the role, acting as if you had been hired to perform this role in a movie or play. The more you behave exactly as if you already had the habit, the more you actually become the person that you desire to be.
6. Tell others that you have decided to develop this habit. When you tell others, you motivate and encourage yourself. You also force yourself to consistently act in accordance with your new resolutions because you know that others are watching.
7. Continually review your progress on a day-to-day basis. When Benjamin Franklin developed his own process for character formation, he would review his behaviour every single day to see if he was living consistent with the values that he had determined were important.

You can do the same thing. At the end of every day, do a brief recap of your behaviour during the day relative to the values and habits you are trying to develop. Give yourself points when you are strong and be patient with yourself when you slip from time-to-time.

The most important keys to developing new habit patterns are patience, determination and persistence. When you begin to change yourself, you will find that it is not particularly easy. But it is possible if you continue to work at it.

You can take complete control over the shaping of your character and personality and everything that happens to you in the future, by making the decision, right now, to define and develop the habits that will lead you to great success.

And when you develop the habits possessed by other successful people, you will enjoy an equal, if not greater, level of success.

FORMULA FOR FAILURE AND SUCCESS

Failure is not a single, cataclysmic event.

We do not fail overnight.

Failure is the inevitable result of an accumulation of poor thinking and poor choices. To put it more simply, failure is nothing more than a few errors in judgment repeated every day.

Now why would someone make an error in judgment and then be so foolish as to repeat it every day? The answer is because he or she does not think that it matters.

On their own, our daily acts do not seem that important. A minor oversight, a poor decision or a wasted hour generally doesn't result in an instant and measurable impact. More often than not, we escape from any immediate consequences of our deeds.

If we have not bothered to read a single book in the past ninety days, this lack of discipline does not seem to have any immediate impact on our lives.

And since nothing drastic happened to us after the first ninety days, we repeat this error in judgment for another ninety days and on and on it goes. Why? Because it doesn't seem to matter. And herein lies the great danger. Far worse than not reading the books is not even realizing that it matters!

Those who eat too many of the wrong foods are contributing to a future health problem, but the joy of the moment overshadows the consequence of the future. It does not seem to matter.

Those who smoke too much or drink too much go on making these poor choices year after year... because it doesn't seem to matter. But the pain and regret of these errors in judgment have only been delayed for a future time.

Consequences are seldom instant; instead, they accumulate until the inevitable day of reckoning finally arrives and the price must be paid for our poor choices–choices that didn't seem to matter.

Failure's most dangerous attribute is its subtlety. In the short term those little errors don't seem to make any difference. We do not seem to be failing.

In fact, sometimes these accumulated errors in judgment occur throughout a period of great joy and prosperity in our lives.

Since nothing terrible happens to us, since there are no instant consequences to capture our attention, we simply drift from one day to the next, repeating the errors, thinking the wrong thoughts, listening to the wrong voices and making the wrong choices.

The sky did not fall in on us yesterday; therefore the act was probably harmless. Since it seemed to have no measurable consequence, it is probably safe to repeat.

But we must become better educated than that!

If at the end of the day when we made our first error in judgment the sky had fallen in on us, we undoubtedly would have taken immediate steps to ensure that the act would never be repeated again.

Like the child who places his hand on a hot burner despite his parents' warnings, we would have had an instantaneous experience accompanying our error in judgment.

Unfortunately, failure does not shout out its warnings as our parents once did. This is why it is imperative to refine our philosophy in order to be able to make better choices.

With a powerful, personal philosophy guiding our every step, we become more aware of our errors in judgment and more aware that each error really does matter.

Now here is the great news. Just like the formula for failure, the formula for success is easy to follow: It's a few simple disciplines practised every day.

Now here is an interesting question worth pondering: How can we change the errors in the formula for failure into the disciplines required in the formula for success? The answer is by making the future an important part of our current philosophy.

Both success and failure involve future consequences, namely the inevitable rewards or unavoidable regrets resulting from past activities. If this is true, why don't more people take time to ponder the future?

The answer is simple: They are so caught up in the current moment that it doesn't seem to matter. The problems and the rewards of today are so absorbing to some human beings that they never pause long enough to think about tomorrow.

But what if we did develop a new discipline to take just a few minutes every day to look a little further down the road? We would then be able to foresee the impending consequences of our current conduct.

Armed with that valuable information, we would be able to take the necessary action to change our errors into new success-oriented disciplines.

In other words, by disciplining ourselves to see the future in advance, we would be able to change our thinking, amend our errors and develop new habits to replace the old.

One of the exciting things about the formula for success–a few simple disciplines practised every day—is that the results are almost immediate.

As we voluntarily change daily errors into daily disciplines, we experience positive results in a very short period of time. When we change our diet, our health improves noticeably in just a few weeks.

When we start exercising, we feel a new vitality almost immediately. When we begin reading, we experience a growing awareness and a new level of self-confidence.

Whatever new discipline we begin to practise daily will produce exciting results that will drive us to become even better at developing new disciplines.

The real magic of new disciplines is that they will cause us to amend our thinking. If we were to start today to read the books, keep a journal, attend the classes, listen more and observe more, then today would be the first day of a new life leading to a better future.

If we were to start today to try harder and in every way make a conscious and consistent effort to change subtle and deadly errors into constructive and rewarding disciplines, we would never again settle for a life of existence–not once we have tasted the fruits of a life of substance!

REAL ACTION

The world seems to belong to those who reach out and grab it with both hands. It belongs to those who do something rather than just wish and hope and plan and pray and intend to do something someday, when everything is just right. Successful people are not necessarily those who make the right decisions all the time. No one can do that, no matter how smart he is.

But once successful people have made a decision, they begin moving toward their objectives step-by-step and they begin to get feedback or signals to tell them where they're off course and when course corrections are necessary.

As they take action and move toward their goals, they continually get new information that enables them to adjust their plans in large and small ways.

It's important to understand that life is a series of approximations and course adjustments. Let me explain...

When an aeroplane leaves Chicago for Los Angeles, it is off course 99 percent of the time. This is normal and natural and to be expected. The pilot makes continual course corrections, a little to the north, a little to the south. The pilot continually adjusts altitude and throttle.

And sure enough, several hours later, the plane touches down at exactly the time predicted when it first became airborne upon leaving Chicago. The entire journey has been a process of approximations and course adjustments.

What's the big problem? The big problem is that there are no guarantees in life. Everything you do, even crossing the street, is filled with uncertainty.

You can never be completely sure that any action or behaviour is going to bring about the desired result. There is always a risk. And where there is risk, there is fear. And whatever you think about grows in your mind and heart.

People who think continually about the risks involved in any undertaking soon become pre-occupied with fears and doubts and anxieties that conspire to hold them back from trying in the first place.

At Babson College, in a 12-year study into the reasons for success, researchers concluded that virtually all success was based on what they called the "corridor principle." They likened achieving success to proceeding down a corridor in life.

Each of us stands at the entrance to this corridor, looking into the darkness and we see the corridor disappear into the distance. The researchers said that the difference between the successes and the failures in their study could be summarised by the one word–launch!

Successful people were willing to launch themselves down the corridor of opportunity without any guarantee of what would occur. They were willing to risk uncertainty and overcome the normal fears and doubts that hold the great majority in place.

And the remarkable thing is that as you move down the corridor of life, new doors of opportunity open up on both sides of you. However, you would not have seen those doors if you had not moved down the corridor. They would not have opened up for you if you had waited for some assurance before stepping out in faith and taking action.

The Confucian saying "A journey of a thousand leagues begins with a single step" simply means that great accomplishments begin with your willingness to face the inevitable uncertainty of any new enterprise and step out boldly in the direction of your goal.

Not long ago, a couple came to me with a problem. He was working for a company owned by his family in which he was bitterly unhappy. It was full of politics and backbiting and negativity and he was stressed out and hated his job. He wanted to do something else but had no job offers or potential alternatives to his current position. He asked me for my advice on what to do.

I explained to him that there is a "vacuum theory of prosperity," which says that when you create a vacuum of any kind, nature rushes to fill it.

In his case, this meant that as long as he stayed at his current job, there was no way that he could recognise other possibilities and there was no way that other opportunities could find him. I told him to take a giant leap of faith and just walk away from his current job with no lifeline or safety net.

I assured him that if he did, all kinds of things would open up for him that he simply couldn't see while he was locked up in his current situation. He took my advice. He quit his job. The members of his family became very angry and told him that he would be unemployable outside of their business.

But he stuck to his guns. He went home, took a few days off and began to think about his experience and his skills and how they could best be applied to other jobs in other companies.

Within two weeks, without raising a finger, he had two job offers from other companies, both paying substantially more than he was getting before and both offering all kinds of opportunities that were vastly superior to the job he had walked away from.

As soon as the word had got out in the marketplace that he was available, other company owners, having worked with him and his company in the past, were eager to open doors for him.

As he moved down the corridor of life, he began to see possibilities that he had been missing completely by limiting himself to where he was.

If you want to be more successful faster, just do or try more things. Take more action; get busier. Start a little earlier; work a little harder; stay a little later. Put the odds in your favour.

According to the Law of Probability, the more things you try, the more likely it is that you will try the one thing that will make all the difference. I've found that luck is quite predictable. If you want more luck, take more chances. Be more active. Show up more often.

Tom Peters, the best-selling author of In Search of Excellence and other business books, found that a key quality of the top executives in his study was a "bias for action."

Their motto seemed to be, "Ready, aim, fire." Their attitude toward business was summarised in the words, "Do it, fix it, try it." They realised that the future belongs to the action-oriented, to the risk taker.

Top people know, as General Douglas MacArthur once said, "There is no security in life, only opportunity." And the interesting thing is this: If you seek for opportunity, you'll end up with all the security you need.

However, if you seek for security, you'll end up with neither opportunity nor security. The proof of this is all around us, in the downsizing and reconstructing of corporations, where thousands of men and women who sought security are finding themselves unemployed for long periods of time.

There is a "momentum principle of success," which is very important to you. It's derived from two physical laws, the Law of Momentum and the Law of Inertia and it applies equally well to everything that you accomplish and fail to accomplish.

In Physics, the Law of Momentum says that a body in motion tends to remain in motion unless acted upon by an outside force. The Law of Inertia, on the other hand, says that a body at rest tends to remain at rest unless acted upon by an outside force.

In their simplest terms, as they apply to you and your life, those laws say that if you stay in motion toward something that is important to you, it's much easier to continue making progress than it is if you stop somewhere along the way and have to start again.

When you look at successful people, you find that they are very much like the plate spinners in the circus. They get things started; they get the plates spinning. They continually keep them spinning, knowing that if a plate falls off or something comes to a halt, it's much harder to get it restarted than it is to keep it going in the first place.

Once you have a goal and a plan, get going! And once you start moving toward your goal, don't stop. Do something every day to move you closer toward your goal. Don't let the size of the goal or the amount of time required to accomplish it phase you or hold you back.

During your planning process, break down the goal into small tasks and activities that you can engage in every day.

You don't have to do a lot, but every day, every week, every month you should be making progress, by completing your pre-determined tasks and activities, in the direction of your clearly defined objectives.

And here's where the rubber meets the road. The most important single quality for success is self-discipline. It's the ability to make yourself do what you should do, when you should do it, whether you feel like it or not.

Let me break down that definition of self-discipline.

First, it's the ability to make yourself. This means that you have to use strength and willpower to force yourself into motion, to break the power of inertia that holds you back.

Second, do what you should do, when you should do it. This means that you make a plan, set a schedule and then do what you say you'll do. You do it when you say you'll do it. You keep your promises to yourself and to others.

The third part of this definition is whether you feel like it or not. You see, anyone can do anything if he feels like it, if he wants to do it because it makes him happy, if he is well-rested and has lots of time.

However, the true test of character is when you do something that you know you must do whether you feel like it or not, especially when you don't like it at all.

In fact, you can tell how badly you really want something and what you're really made of as a person, by how capable you are of taking action in the direction of your goals and dreams even when you feel tired and discouraged and disappointed and you don't seem to be making any progress. And very often, this is the exact time when you will break through to great achievement.

Ralph Waldo Emerson once wrote, "When the night is darkest, the stars come out." Your ability to endure, to continue taking action, step-by-step, in the direction of your dreams, is what will ultimately assure your success. If you keep on keeping on, nothing can stop you.

PREPARING FOR FUTURE

Earl Nightingale once said that if a person does not prepare for his success, when his opportunity comes, it will only make him look foolish. You've probably heard it said repeatedly that luck is what happens when preparedness meets opportunity.

Only when you've paid the price to be ready for your success are you in a position to take advantage of your opportunities when they arise. And the most remarkable thing is this: The very act of preparation attracts to you, like iron filings to a magnet, opportunities to use that preparation to advance in your life.

You'll seldom learn anything of value or prepare yourself in any area, without soon having a chance to use your new knowledge and your new skills to move ahead more rapidly.

There is a series of things that you can do to become ready for success. All of these activities require self-discipline and a good deal of faith. They require self-discipline because the most normal and natural thing for people to do is to try to get by without preparation.

Instead of taking the time and making the effort to be ready for their chance when it comes, they fool around, listen to the radio, watch television and then they try to wing it and dupe others into thinking that they are more prepared than they really are.

And since we're all transparent, since just about everyone can see through just about everyone else, the unprepared person simply looks incompetent and foolish.

Preparation also requires a lot of faith because you have no proof in advance to demonstrate that the preparation will pay off. You simply have to believe, deep within yourself, that everything you do of a constructive nature will come back to you in some way.

You have to know that no good effort is ever wasted. You have to be willing to sow for a long time before you reap, knowing that if you do sow in quality and quantity, the reaping will come about inevitably with the force of a law of nature.

Look at your work. Be honest and objective about your strengths and weaknesses.

What are you good at? What are you poor at? What is your major area of weakness? What must you absolutely, positively be excellent at in order to move to the top of your field? What one skill do you have that, because of its weakness, may be holding you back from using all your other skills?

Norman Augustine, CEO of Martin Marietta Corporation, recently said that the most important thing he learned in the last 10 years of business was that your weakest important skill determines the extent to which you can use all of your other talents and abilities.

In looking at the hundreds of people who worked below him in his corporation, he had found that people's careers were largely determined not only by their strengths but also by their weaknesses.

The very act of overcoming a particular weakness, through preparation and practise, was enough to propel a person into the front ranks in his or her career.

In preparing for success, one of the very best questions that you can ask yourself, continually, is: "What can I and only I do that, if done well, will make a real difference in my career?"

Usually, there is only one or perhaps two answers to that question. Your ability to honestly appraise yourself and to identify the particular skill area that may be holding you back is critical.

Remember when I said that preparation requires both self-discipline and faith.

It requires self-discipline because your natural tendency is to do more and more of those things that come most easily to you and to avoid those areas that you don't enjoy because you're not particularly good at them yet.

It requires faith and character for you to admit your weaknesses in a particular area and then resolve to go to work to develop yourself so those weaknesses don't hold you back.

The greatest change that has taken place in our society in the last 20 years is that it's become an information based society. More than 50 per cent of the working population is in the business of processing information in some way.

This means that we now have a knowledge-based society and that you're a knowledge worker. You work with your mind, your brain, your mental talents and abilities.

You no longer "load that bale and tote that hay." You work by thinking and the more effectively you think and the better prepared you are mentally, the more productive and positive you'll be.

One thing that has helped me enormously over the years is the habit of getting up early in the morning and spending the first 30 to 60 minutes reading something uplifting. You can read material that is educational or motivational or even inspirational. Many people read spiritual literature.

Henry Ward Beecher once said, "The first hour is the rudder of the day." This is often called the "golden hour." It's the hour during which you programme your mind and set your emotional tone for the rest of the day.

If you get up in the morning at least two hours before you have to be at work or before your first appointment and spend the first hour investing in your mind, taking in "mental protein" rather than "mental candy," reading good books rather than the newspaper or magazines, your whole day will flow more smoothly.

You'll be more positive and optimistic. You'll be calmer, more confident and relaxed. You'll have a greater sense of control and well-being by the very act of reading healthy material for the first hour of each day.

After just three days of reading for 30 to 60 minutes in the morning, you'll notice a profound difference. You'll begin to develop what Dr. William Glasser called a "positive addiction."

As a result of your early-morning reading, you'll feel so good about yourself and your life that you'll develop a desire and motivation to get up earlier, even though your tendency in the past was to sleep in later.

Try it and see. It's a wonderful experience and it can have a profound impact on the rest of your life.

In the period of time before work, another thing that highly successful people do is plan and prepare for their entire day.

They review all of the tasks and responsibilities that they have for the coming hours. They carefully make a list of all their activities and they set clear priorities on the activities. They decide which things are most important to do, which are secondary in importance and which things should not be done at all unless all the other things are finished.

They then discipline themselves to start working on their most important tasks and stay with them during the day until they're complete. Again, the natural tendency of the low performer is to do what is fun and easy before he does what is hard and necessary.

Underachievers always like to do the little things first. They are drawn to the tasks that contribute very little to their careers or future possibilities.

But high achievers are not like that! High achievers discipline themselves to start at the top of their list and to work on the activities in order of importance, without diversion or distraction.

If you're in sales, you should spend fully 80 per cent of your time prospecting until you're so busy with presentations and proposals that you've no time left to prospect at all.

In fact, whenever you have money problems of any kind, you should look upon them as a signal telling you that you need to reorder your priorities and to prepare more thoroughly to accomplish more of the things that contribute the greatest value to your life.

Another way to prepare for success is to eat right. Energy and dynamism are essential to your success and they're possible only when you're sharp and alert.

There are foods that are highly nutritious and that give you high energy and vitality on through the day. Also, there are foods, which you eat usually by habit, that are hard for your system to digest and that tire you out and make you slow and drowsy in the morning and the afternoon.

The chief culprits in diets are foods containing fats of any kind. More and more nutritional research suggests that fatty foods, which require the greatest effort on the part of the body to break down and digest, are the real enemies of human performance.

Fats are becoming closely linked to many illnesses and ailments. One reason why people drink so much coffee is to counteract the drowsiness that occurs naturally in the morning because their stomachs are so loaded down with fatty foods.

You see, the process of digestion is the activity of your body that consumes the most energy. When you eat foods that are hard to digest, your body rushes blood from everywhere to the digestive system to work to break them down.

In this process, the digestive system draws away blood from the brain and the muscles. The reason you feel drowsy after a large meal is because the blood has gone from your brain to your stomach.

The reason you get cramps when you engage in vigorous physical exercise immediately after eating is because a substantial amount of blood has been drawn from your muscles to aid in the process of digestion.

The key is to eat lightly and healthily. Eat more fruits and vegetables. Eat more whole-grain products.

In his book Eat to Win, Robert Haas says that your diet should be comprised of 75 percent carbohydrates, 15 per cent fats and only 10 percent proteins.

Since the average diet in America contains as much as 50 per cent fats and proteins, there is ample room to improve. And every move that you make toward a high-carbohydrate diet will give you more energy and make you sharper in everything you do.

In preparing for success throughout the day, you should also talk to yourself in a positive way. The work by Dr. Martin Seligman at the University of Pennsylvania has demonstrated that the way you talk to yourself largely determines your emotions, how you feel about yourself on a minute-to-minute basis.

If you don't deliberately and consciously think about what you want and talk to yourself in a positive way, your mind will tend to slip toward your worries and your concerns. And negative thinking takes the edge off your personality and your enthusiasm, which is so important to your success with people.

A few years ago, Dr. Abraham Zaleznik of Harvard University did an interesting study on disappointment. He found that successful people bounce back from disappointments far faster than unsuccessful people do.

And what I've learned is that the key to your keeping yourself positive and optimistic is preparation in advance of the ups and downs that You'll experience each day.

For example, if you're in sales, change the way you talk to yourself by viewing yourself as a "rejection specialist" rather than a "sales specialist." If you define yourself as a sales specialist, you'll be setting yourself up for failure, disappointment and lowered self-esteem with every rejection you get.

But, on the other hand, if you look upon yourself as a rejection specialist, you'll be setting yourself up to feel like a winner every time someone turns you down for any reason. You can look upon every rejection as a percentage of a sale.

If it takes you 20 calls to make a sale, you can look upon a rejection as 5 per cent of the commission that you receive for making that sale. In this way, every person you speak to actually pays you money.

You simply collect it when you make the sale that is inevitable when you speak to enough people. Every time someone turns you down, you're a winner. You're just that much farther ahead. You're just a little bit closer to the sale that must come if you keep on keeping on.

Use every setback or disappointment as a spur to greater effort. Decide that nothing will ever get you down. Decide that you will bounce back instead of break. Develop a resilient or hardy personality.

Become the kind of person who is always cheerful, no matter what happens on the outside. Develop an attitude of gratitude and give thanks for everything that happens to you, knowing that every step forward is a step toward achieving something bigger and better than your current situation.

In this way, you become a far more resourceful and effective person. Preparing mentally, you become almost un-stoppable.

If you're making sales calls, resist the "parking-lot mentality" of the average salesperson. The average salesperson doesn't think about the client until he drives onto the parking lot and he stops thinking about the client when he drives off.

Instead, prepare thoroughly for each call. Review your file of notes on the customer and establish a clear set of call objectives before you go in. Know what you're doing and why. Be very clear on what you want to accomplish with this call.

If a person were to ask you how you would judge whether or not this upcoming call was successful, you should be able to tell that person exactly what you want to accomplish and after the call, you should be able to tell that person exactly what you achieved.

Most sales-people never do this. When you ask them if a call was successful, they don't know how to answer you or how to base it. But this is not for you.

In everything you do, preparation is the key. If you want to be ready for success, you have to plant the seeds well in advance of the harvest that you expect.

Do what the winners do: Think on paper. Memorise the winner's creed: "Everything counts."

Everything you do is either moving you toward your goals or moving you away. Everything is either helping you or hurting you. Nothing is neutral. Everything counts.

A successful businessman was once asked for advice by a young person on how he could be more successful faster. The businessman told him that the key to his success had been to "get good" at his job.

The young man said, "I'm already good at what I do."

The businessman then said, "Well, get better!"

The young man, somewhat self-satisfied, said, "Well, I'm already better than most people."

To that, the businessman replied, "Then be the best."

Those are three of the best pieces of advice I've ever heard:

Get good. Get better. Be the best!

Remember, we live in a knowledge-based society and knowledge in every field is doubling approximately every seven years. This means that you must double your knowledge in your field every seven years just to stay even.

You've already "made out" at your current level of knowledge and skill. You've reached the ceiling in your career with your current talents and abilities.

If you want to go faster and farther, you must get back to work and begin to prepare yourself for greater heights.

You must put aside the newspaper, turn off the television, politely excuse yourself from aimless socialising and get back to working on yourself.

A quotation by Abraham Lincoln had a great influence on my life when I was 15. It was a statement he made when he was a young lawyer in Springfield, Illinois. He said, "I will study and prepare myself and someday my chance will come."

If you study and prepare yourself, your chance will come as well. There is nothing that you cannot accomplish if you'll invest the effort to get yourself ready for the success that you desire.

And there is nothing that can stop you but your own lack of preparation. Let me end with this beautiful poem by Henry Wordsworth Longfellow:

> *"Those heights by great men won and kept; Were not achieved by sudden flight; But they, while their companions slept; Were toiling upward in the night"*

Your possibilities are endless, your potential is unlimited and your future opens up before you when you prepare yourself for the success that must inevitably be yours.

Zarathushtrian Formula for Success

I would like to share the main guiding principles of the religion of Zarathushtra. In the Gathas, Asho Zarathushtra lays out a simple, yet profound, guide for living our life. These are very specific things that we can work on incorporating in our life to achieve success in our life. If we inculcate these concepts, we can empower ourselves to change our lives and begin to be on the road to Success. These are very simple things to do in our day to day life. But because they are simple, they are also very simple not to do in our daily lives.

First and foremost, we must believe, respect and adore the Supreme Creator with Infinite Wisdom—Ahura Mazda, Hormazd.

Second, we must actively work to develop our Good Mind–Behman (Vohuman). To succeed in this life, we must have a burning desire within us to do so. We must want to be somebody. Be a future thinker. Think about what can happen in the future and set difficult yet realistic goals for 3 months, 6 months, 1yr, 3yrs, 5yrs from today. Have goals that motivate us and make us stretch to reach them. We must have a Big Dream. The dream must be something that is very important to us. Have a big dream and then have a plan to pursue that dream. Develop a positive winning attitude.

Third, we must inculcate Ardebehest –Asha in our daily life. Asha is Righteousness and Divine Order. We must always speak the Truth. We must always do what is Right. Our reputation is everything. Do what is right and stand for what we believe in. We do not want to be average and ordinary. We are born in this world to make a difference. We have to be tough to succeed.

Fourth principle to practise is Shehrevar—work hard to help others. Work hard and live right. Be passionate for what we can do for others. Having developed a positive attitude, we need to generate benevolent activity. Do good deeds. Help others. Live a life of self sacrifice. If we help others, we get Khashathraa–the Power of God, to do more and more Good for others.

Fifth principle is spendarmad or Spenta Aaaramaiti. We must develop faith in Ahura Mazda, an unflinching faith in our religion and its teachings. This faith will help us to fulfil our dream. We must develop a positive attitude about life. No one likes a dull, disillusioned, depressing, dogged cry-baby. If we just like something, we will never be good at something. We must love what we do and not just like what we do. We have to love it with a passion. Whatever we do, we must make a total commitment. All we can control is our attitude and our activity.

The Gathas teach us that if we incorporate the above five sequences in our daily life then our soul (Urvan) will begin to experience the consequences of Khordaad and Amerdaad– Perfection and Immortality.

Zarathushtra's formula for success is:

Hormazd + Behman + Ardebehest + Shehrevar + Spenta Aaramaiti = Khordaad + Amerdaad.

We have a tendency to put successful persons on a pedestal. I want to stress to you that each and every one of us has the same potential. If we want to be successful in reaching our dream, we've got to learn to work hard. We've got to learn to do the right thing. We've got to do our best. We've got to give it our all. All we can do is all we can do. All we can do is everything. Right? God should come first, family second and work or business should come third. Only when we get our priorities in order, we have a chance to be all the person we want to be.

People want to feel good. Praise and reward others at every chance that we get. Empower them so that they can function to their full capacity. Don't let anyone tell us that we can not do what we want to do. Life don't give us what we want. Life don't give us what we love to have. Life gives us what we will accept. Life gives us what we will fight for. If we accept to be average and ordinary, then that's what we will be.

We will have difficulties in our life, failures in our life. In our life things are not going to work right all the time. We must never quit. We must pay the price in building this mental toughness. When we fail, we should not give up. We must fail forward. We must be able to pick it up and go for it one more time. Refuse to be rejected and learn to reject the rejection. The only thing standing between us and our dreams is our willingness to do the things that we need to do. Focus on doing that and be consistent and persistent.

Let today be the new beginning for the rest of our life. We are the captain of our ship. We are the Masters of our Destiny. Let us Empower ourselves. Let us make a decision to totally and completely change our life for the service of our community in the days to come. Almost everybody gets there, almost everybody is over the hump, almost everybody has it going, almost everybody is the way of life to almost everybody, But the winners they do it. What do they do? They do whatever it takes to get the job done. They do good deeds. They help others. They live a life of self sacrifice. They do it and do it and do it until they reach their goals.

We are here for a flicker, time is running out. Let us have a sense of urgency and let us do it and do it and do it and do it and do it and do it and do it and do it until we reach our goal of Perfection and Immortality.

❑

4

STRESS MANAGEMENT

HEALTH

Physical Fitness: Any time a person changes his or her level of activity, risks are involved. This is especially true if a person has a physical disability such as a spinal cord injury or heart disease. It is important that trainers emphasise that students check with a physician before starting an exercise programme.

Objectives

1. Identify the benefits of being physically active.
2. Identify three ways that you can become more physically active.

Instructional Format: A lesson on physical fitness should be fun. Most people know that being physically active is vital to good health. Nevertheless, using that knowledge is easier said than done; so, people need motivation. "Fitness" tends to conjure up images of five mile runs an hours in a weight room.

Adopting a physically active lifestyle does not have to require much time or effort. This is especially true for people who are extremely sedentary. A slight increase in a person's activity level can lead to significant benefits. Instead of a "no pain, no gain" approach, this lesson will take an "every little bit helps" approach.

1. Discuss the benefits of fitness. Most people will know about losing weight, but other benefits are outlined

below. It is important for people to realise that being physically fit and being thin are not always inclusive. A person who is thin but does not exercise may have low energy, clogged arteries and trouble concentrating at work. On the other hand, a person with 10-20 kgs of extra fat can have a strong heart and excellent stamina at work due to regular exercise. However, it is important to keep in mind that a person who is overweight, regardless of his fitness level, is at risk for health problems. The information below is based on an Internet article by John Abdo. The article is titled "The Benefits of Fitness."

- Increasing fitness improves energy. People may disagree with this statement, especially after they start an exercise programme and they are sore, tired and ready to quit. Inform the students that once they adopt a more physically active lifestyle, they will slowly begin to feel better, their bodies will tend to burn fat better and they will lose weight. Additionally, this increased energy transfers into being more productive at work and at home.
- Increasing fitness helps a person think better when under stress. Use the following information to explain this complex process. When we are under stress, our heart beats faster, we may start to sweat and we may breath harder. If our bodies are not used to those changes, we tend to have a hard time thinking and handling the pressure. When we are physically active, the same changes in our bodies take place. If we are having fun and thinking while we are active, then our bodies get practise for dealing with the increased heart rate, breathing, etc. Also, the more fit a person is, the more activity is needed to make these

changes in the body. Therefore, when a person gets in a stressful situation, a fit body is not going to react as dramatically as an unfit body. An improved mind and ability to handle stress will definitely improve work performance.

- Increasing fitness improves muscles and bones. This benefit is obvious. For students who have jobs that require physical exertion, strong muscles and bones lead to improved performance and a decrease chance for injury.
- Increasing fitness improves the heart and lungs. If your heart and lungs are accustomed to physical activity, it is not going to seem like the end of the world when you need to go up a flight of stairs, walk more than a mile or lift a few heavy boxes.
- Increased fitness improves your looks. As mentioned previously, improving your fitness may not lead to the body of a super model. However, toning muscles and losing fat may help a person drop a few inches around the waist and look more healthy. This may give a person more confidence to continue engaging in exercise. People who are obese tend to feel uncomfortable when exercising, which leads to decreased motivation. Remember, every little bit helps.

2. Discuss ways a person can increase his physical activity. There are several things to consider when a person is planning to increase his activity level by starting an exercise programme. A person will need to figure out where he will exercise, what equipment he might need, when he will exercise and how to do the exercise properly. A health club would help answer these questions, but most students are not going to be able afford membership to a club. The information below should give some guidance for

those who need and/or want to increase their activity levels.

- Before discussing some specifics of exercise, review these principles of exercise outlined by Dale Bogle.

  Progression: Start slow and gradually increase. A person should consult a doctor before beginning.

  Regularity: Try to exercise at least three times a week.

  Overload: To obtain the maximum benefit, you should exceed normal demands placed on the body. *For example,* if a person can walk a mile with little problem, she may have to walk faster or longer.

  Variety: Doing the same exercise day after day can ruin motivation. Try to spice things up.

  Recovery: Take a day after taxing a group of muscles. This principle usually applies to running and lifting weights.

  Balance: Make sure to include the 3 components of exercise below.

  Specificity: Set goals and design exercise to meet those goals. If you want to run a 5K race, you should run instead of ride a bike.

- The first component of fitness is cardiorespiratory. This is achieved through aerobic exercise. Aerobic exercise refers to exercise that keeps the heart beating at a higher rate than normal for an extended period of time (20-30 minutes). This is the easiest type of exercise because all that is really required is a good pair of shoes. Taking a 30 minutes walk three times a week is all that is needed to burn fat and lead to other health benefits. Other aerobic activities that require more equipment and/or a special place to do it include running, biking, aerobics and swimming. Playing sports like tennis and basketball can also provide some aerobic benefit.

- The second component of fitness is strength and muscular endurance. A person who has more muscle is going to burn more calories. This means that adding muscle will help even when a person is lying down. Strength training usually requires weights. However, a person can do push-ups and sit-ups to obtain some of the benefit of weight training. There are many different types of exercise a person can do to increase strength. If there are students who are genuinely interested in starting a strength programme, a trainer may want to contact a fitness trainer in the area to see if she would be willing to provide additional instruction. Alternatively, there may be classes offered through different community agencies that a student could attend. There are also several fitness programmes on television that can be taped.
- The final component of fitness is flexibility. Flexibility is improved by doing basic stretching. Flexible muscles and joints are less likely to get injured while engaging in physical activity. There are several types of flexibility exercises and they often are part of aerobics or strength training. Use similar resources mentioned with strength training to teach specific flexibility exercises.

3. The information contained in number 2 dealt specifically with exercise programmes, but there are many ways a person can become more active without engaging in a fitness programme. Ask the students if they can think of any.
    - Use stairs instead of the elevator.

- Park in a place that requires you to walk farther.
- Walk or ride a bike to work.
- Walk to the next bus stop.
- Go window shopping (but do not stop to look very long).
- Take a dog for a walk.
- Use your 15-minutes break at work to go for a walk.
- Do a few push-ups or sit-ups during commercials.
- House work and yard work burn calories.

NUTRITION

Objectives

1. Identify the major dietary guidelines from the Centre for Nutrition Policy and Promotion.
2. Identify the benefits of maintaining a well-balanced diet.

Instructional Format: This lesson will provide information on how to eat properly. There will be no information on dieting, *per se*. Rather, eating properly should be taught in the context of being healthy and how that improved health is important for job performance. Information from the lesson titled "Fitness" and providing information on reducing calories in this lesson should give people enough information on losing weight. The information on the Food Guide Pyramid is from the Centre for Nutrition Policy and Promotion, which is an agency within the United States Department of Agriculture.

1. Meet with the members of the class for a short introductory session. During this meeting, the trainer should introduce the lesson and instruct the students that they should keep track of the food and beverages they consume each day for a week. Give them the recording form that is provided. For students who

have difficulty writing, instruct them to have someone help them record what they eat. If this assignment is too difficult for most of the class members, skip this step and adjust the lesson accordingly.

2. Using the information contained in the materials on the Food Guide Pyramid, provide instruction on how to maintain a balanced diet. Use visual aids as needed. Discuss each of the six different food groups, what foods are in each group and about how much they should have from each group each day. Providing information on the exact amount of servings that are recommended may get too complex for many students, so try to provide general guidelines. *For example,* "it is important that you eat more servings from the bread group than the meat group. Try to eat a few fruits and vegetables each day and very little fat or sugar."
3. Discuss calorie intake. Calories are the fuel that the body needs to burn to provide energy. Energy allows us to be more productive, alert and think better. If people are getting their "energy" from sugar, nicotine and caffeine, they should be informed that this provides short-term "energy" which requires continued consumption of these products to keep that false sense of energy. In order to have "good energy," a person needs to consume healthy calories. This is accomplished by eating 2,000-3,000 healthy calories throughout the day. People should eat breakfast, lunch and dinner with a few healthy snacks in between.

   Counting calories can be complex and tedious, so use the information provided to teach some basic guidelines. People get their calories from three basic sources: carbohydrates, protein and fats. There is much debate about what percentage of a person's daily intake should come from each source of calories. Most guidelines suggest that 50-60 percent of your calories should come from carbohydrates (breads, grain, fruits and vegetables) and the other 40-50 per cent should come from protein (cheese, meat, milk) and fat (butter, lard, oil). Instruct students that a person gets more energy when she burns calories from carbohydrates and protein. Yet, fat contains twice as many calories per gram as the other two. By eating a greater percentage of carbohydrates and protein, the person gets more energy from fewer calories.

Remind students that they still need to be concerned with calories. If you consume 3,000 healthy calories a day and only burn 2,500 calories, you are still going to gain weight. Nevertheless, use the following example to stress that eating properly allows a person to consume more food and still be healthy. If a person starts the day with a sausage biscuit with egg at a local fast food place, he has just consumed more than a fourth of the recommended calories (560) and over half the recommended fat (35 grams). This means that he has used up quite a bit of his daily allowance on a little, probably unsatisfying breakfast. A bowl of breakfast food, banana and glass of juice would provide the person more energy from fewer calories and almost no fat. This would allow the person to put a little extra mayonnaise or cheese on his sandwich at lunch and still meet his daily requirement of calories and fat. It is important to stress balance. Having a Big Mac® every once in a while is not going to be a big deal. The idea is to get students to adopt a lifestyle that includes a well-balanced diet most of the time.

4. Discuss that a well-balanced diet also is important for other health concerns. When it comes to nutrition, people generally think only about body weight. However, a person who is thin and eating a lot of

fatty foods is putting himself at risk of having health problems such as high blood pressure and high cholesterol, which can lead to heart attacks. Some people have medical conditions, such as diabetes, that require them to follow a strict diet. It is important to stress the importance of following a doctor's recommended diet. When a person does not do that, he puts himself at risk for serious health problems. Remind people that it is hard to be successful at work when they are using many sick days due to illness that can be prevented by a proper diet.

5. In order to review some of the concepts discussed, review the nutritional contents of different food products. This will also provide training on how to read food labels. Some important figures to look at include the serving size, number of calories from fat compared to the total calories and percentage of the daily allowance from fat, cholesterol, sodium, carbohydrates and protein. A healthy food should have a small percentage of its calories from fat, little to no saturated fat, cholesterol and sodium. Try to find foods that contribute more than 25 per cent of the daily recommended allowance of fat, cholesterol or sodium in one serving. These foods will help illustrate that sometimes eating a small amount of tasty food can put a huge dent into the total amount of nutrients a person should eat each day. Point out serving sizes. The amount of calories in a bag of chips might be reasonable based on its serving size. However, if the serving size is three chips, it only takes a few handfuls before the amount of calories is unreasonable.
6. For those students who completed a daily food intake form, have them review their information and discuss. Are they eating a healthy diet? What can they do to improve the balance of their diet? Have them look at one meal that was particularly

unhealthy and see if they come up with an alternative, more healthy meal.

CONTROLLING STRESS

Objectives

1. Identify causes of stress.
2. Identify how a body reacts to stress.
3. Identify how not dealing with stress can be harmful.
4. Identify five ways you can cope with stress.

Instructional Format: This part is on stress management will provide basic information about the effects of stress on the body and how to deal with it. Most people understand the word stress. Nevertheless, many do not know how to recognise when they are under stress or how to deal with it. Some of the coping strategies are skills that are taught in other lessons in the manual and some of the skills can be practised. However, many coping strategies will only be discussed. Much of the information contained in this part is based on a book by Sapolsky and a book by Corbin and Lindsey. References are listed below.

1. Define the word "stressor" as the cause of stress. According to Sapolsky, a stressor is anything that throws a body out of its normal state. If a person starts thinking about a test he has to take and his palms start to sweat, his heart rate increases and his stomach feels upset, his normal body state has changed. Thus, thinking about the test is a stressor. If those changes occur while taking the test, taking the test is a stressor.
2. Discuss changes in the body that occur when a person is under stress. Note that these changes are similar to those presented in the social skills unit in the lesson titled "Anger Management." This is because an anger-provoking situation is a stressor. According to Sapolsky and Corbin and Lindsey, a

person's body goes through the following changes when under stress: Increase in the release of stored energy to provide the body more power and stamina, increase in blood flow carrying oxygen to the brain, dilation of the pupils to allow more light to enter the eyes, increase in perspiration, increase in heart rate and blood pressure and decrease in the digestion process. These changes make sense when the stressor is being trapped in a burning building compared to thinking about a test. Yet, the body does not differentiate between stressors. Furthermore, these changes can interfere with a person's performance when the stressor is not life threatening. Examples of this include giving a speech or interviewing for a job. If a person is under stress, his body will have at least some of the reactions to some degree.

3. Discuss different causes of stress. Try to have the students contribute as many causes as possible. The Holmes-Rahe Stress Scale has a list of 43 stressful events. To use the scale, place a check by each event that has occurred in your life over the last 12 months. Then, add the point totals. If you score less than 150, you have a 35 percent chance of illness or accident within the next two years. If you score 150 to 300, you have a 51 percent chance of illness or accident within the next two years. If you score greater than 300, you have an 80 percent chance of illness or accident within the next two years. Take note that stress is not always caused by negative events. Add to the discussion by having students describe, if they remember, how they felt as a result of any of the listed stressors they may have encountered.
4. Discuss the problems associated with not dealing with stress appropriately. Sapolsky points out that some stress in a person's life is useful and expected. However, too much stress alongwith not coping

appropriately can lead to illness. How stress increases the likelihood of illness is complex. Overall, once the body has reacted to stress, it needs to get back to normal. The process of trying to get the body back to its normal state makes it more difficult to fight off infections and cope with a disease. Although it does not guarantee that you will get sick, going through this process repeatedly does increase the likelihood of ulcers, high blood pressure, heart disease and cancer.

5. Discuss coping strategies that can be used for managing stress. Ask the students if they know any coping strategies. Use the handout titled "Ways to Cope with Stress" as a guide. For each strategy, discuss how to do each skill and how the skill might help.

NEGATION OF DESTRUCTIVE BEHAVIOUR

Objective

1. Identify three problems related to drug use and work.

Instructional Format: This lesson will provide information on the problems of drug use specific to health and working. The amount of drug education information that is available is extraordinary. Most people understand that drugs are bad, but do not always think about how the consequences of drug use affect their work.

This lesson is not a substitute for substance abuse treatment. If a person is having difficulties related to the misuse of drugs, he or she should be referred to a trained substance abuse professional.

This training is only designed as an educational programme for job seekers. The drugs that will be discussed in this topic are alcohol, nicotine, caffeine and illicit (marijuana, cocaine, heroine, LSD, etc.) drugs as whole group.

1. Begin the lesson by discussing drug tests at work. Inform students that employers have the right to test for illegal drug use.
    - Seventy-one percent of illegal drug users are employed.
    - Of people who called a cocaine help line, 75 per cent indicated they used drugs while working, 64 percent reported that drugs adversely affected their job performance and 18 percent had stolen from employers to support their drug habit.
    - Drug-using employees at GM average 40 sick days per year compared to 4.5 for non-users.
    - Employees who tested positive on a pre-employment screening at a Utah power company were five times more likely to be involved in a workplace accident.
    - The Institute for Health Policy, out of Brandeis University, found that substance abuse is the number one health problem in the country.
2. Discuss why substance abuse would cost employers so much money.
    - When workers miss work, they need to pay sick days and overtime for replacement workers.
    - Poor performance leads to work not getting done on time and poor quality. When products and services are not done correctly, they need to be done over. Repeating any process costs money.
    - Workplace injuries cost companies a lot of money in prevention programmes, worker's compensation and replacement workers.
    - All of these factors lead to higher turnover. High turnover leads to money being spent on training new employees.
3. Discuss alcohol and illegal drug use. Use of alcohol or illegal drugs while working is definitely related to

poor performance and accidents. Long-term abuse of alcohol or illegal drugs is linked to health problems such as heart disease, cancer and liver disease. Even occasional parting the night before work can impact a person's job. Calling in sick and poor job performance when at work can affect a person's job evaluations and opportunities to advance in the company.

4. Discuss the use of cigarettes and working. All people should be aware about the health dangers of smoking. Nevertheless, students may not think about how smoking affects their job performance. According to information reported on the smoke-free workplace new smokers are absent 50 percent more often than non-smokers and appear to be more unproductive due to frequent smoke breaks. Some evidence also suggests that smoking leads to decreased attentiveness and efficiency. Students should be informed that many companies are implementing strict workplace smoking policies. It is unlikely that a person will be able to smoke whenever or wherever he or she wants on the job.
5. Discuss caffeine and working. There is no substantial link between caffeine use and health or work-related problems. Trainers may want to point out that too much caffeine can interfere with sleep and cause a vicious cycle. The person is tired due to lack of sleep and uses caffeine to stay awake and alert during the day. As mentioned previously, a good night's rest, a proper diet and physical activity can lead to significant health benefits and energy. Remind students that caffeine is a stimulant and can cause nervousness and irritability. Although this may not hurt job performance, it certainly can not help someone deal with the pressures of the job.
6. Discuss unprotected sex and sharing needles as behaviours associated with drug use that can have

serious health consequences. Again, this type of information is available in great detail in many sources and most students probably have heard the information several times. Nevertheless, a reminder in the context of staying healthy would not hurt. Sharing needles when using drugs puts a person at risk of being infected with many diseases, the most serious of which is the Human Immunodeficiency Virus (HIV) that can lead to AIDS. Although having unprotected sex is not directly related to using drugs, a person's judgement is impaired under the influence of drugs or alcohol that can lead to making poor or risky decisions. Having unprotected sex and consequences will be covered more thoroughly in a following lesson titled "Sexually Transmitted Diseases."

APPROPRIATE MEDICAL ADVICE

Objectives

1. Identify different types of health-care services.
2. Identify how to get health insurance to help pay for health care.
3. Identify important information that a person should ask a doctor.
4. Understand the importance of following the directions for taking medications.

Instructional Format: This lesson will cover a broad range of topics to provide the student with information about maximising health-care services. Going to see a doctor is not going to guarantee that a person will get well. You need to know what to ask and follow the directions the doctor gives you. Additionally, you need to be able to pay for these services. It is almost impossible to pay for good healthcare coverage with out-of-pocket money. That is the purpose for the discussion on health insurance.

1. Discuss the importance of seeking medical care when needed. Many people do not go to the doctor because of inconvenience, money and fear. These are all legitimate reasons for avoiding a doctor's office. However, stress to students that putting off seeing a doctor can cause greater inconvenience, money and fear.
2. Discuss available healthcare options in your community. Most insurance companies require that people see a primary care physician before going to a specialist. Inform students that they can go see a specialist any time they want, but they will most likely have to pay for the visit themselves. As a class, go through the Yellow Pages and look up different types of healthcare providers. The best section to look under is "Physicians." This will give a list of physicians by speciality. Most people will go to an internal medicine physician or family practise physician for basic healthcare such as colds, sprains, cuts, etc. Again, people who have health insurance would pick their doctor from a list that the insurance companies provide. Have the students pick out other specialities and discuss what problems those physicians treat. *For example,* a dermatologist treats skin problems, an orthopedist treats injuries to bones, joints and muscles and an opthalmalogist treats problems with eyes.
3. Discuss various healthcare options available in your community. Of course, the clinic where your doctor is located is where you go for basic medical care. Insurance companies usually dictate where a person can go for emergency hospital care. Have students look through the Yellow Pages to identify different hospitals and clinics in the area. Discuss whether there is free medical care available in the community and where it is located. Discuss alternative forms of medical care such as chiropractic therapy,

massage therapy and acupuncture. These are alternative ways to relieve pain and discomfort, especially in the back.

4. Discuss how to get health insurance. Most people get health insurance through their employer. A person who is not eligible for health insurance from any of these sources can purchase health insurance independently through an insurance company. However, the monthly premiums (amount of money the person pays for the insurance) are expensive and coverage is limited. When health insurance is offered through work, the company usually pays part of the premium and the employee pays the rest each month. This will entitle the employee and family, if covered, to seek medical treatment at a significantly reduced cost. Depending on the coverage, the employee may have to pay a certain percentage of the total medical costs, a flat fee for each visit to the doctor or may pay nothing at all. The amount a person pays towards the premium and the amount of coverage a person gets is going to vary tremendously. Common areas in which insurance companies pay most of the cost include: doctor visits, routine diagnostic services (x-ray, blood and urine tests), medical treatment, approved medications, emergency services and hospital costs.
5. When a person goes to a doctor, she has the right to have all medical decisions explained to her. Some doctors do a good job at communicating with patients and some doctors do a poor job. The patient also has a responsibility to explain all health problems and answer all questions from the doctor honestly. The following is a list of information a person should ask a doctor during a doctor's visit.
   - Any time you do not understand something the doctor says, ask her to explain it to you.

- When a doctor indicates that she wants to perform a diagnostic test beyond standard measurements, such as weight, blood pressure and temperature, you can ask what she is looking for when doing an x-ray, blood test or other tests.
- You should ask for the results and an explanation of all diagnostic tests.
- When a doctor gives you a diagnosis, but you do not understand what it means, you can ask the doctor to explain it to you.
- When a doctor tells you to do something to help an ailment, such as applying ice to a sprained ankle, you can ask the doctor that how that will help.
- Any time the doctor gives you an instruction and you do not understand it or need further clarification, ask him to provide more information.
- When a doctor prescribes medication, you can ask: Why? For how long? And what are the side effects? The pharmacist can also answer these questions.
- Before you leave the doctor's room you should make sure that you know whether you need to call the doctor for any test results or need to schedule a follow-up visit.

6. Discuss the importance of following directions for taking medication exactly as written on the label or handout provided. Taking the wrong amount at the wrong time along with certain food or drugs can make the medications completely ineffective. A worst-case scenario of not following the directions is illness or death. The Food and Drug Administration provides the following tips for taking medications safely.
    - If your symptoms are not improving, call your doctor. You may need a different dosage or drug.

Alternatively, the drug may need to be in your system for a while before improvements are noticed.

- If you get any severe side effects, call your doctor. Examples include vomiting, trouble breathing, headaches, rashes and loss of consciousness.
- Do not stop taking medications when you feel better. Follow the advice as to when you should stop.
- Check drug labels for specific instructions such as "take with food" or "do not take with milk."
- Check to see where the medications should be stored.
- Always keep medications out of the reach of children.
- Never let another person take your medication and never take the medication of another person. Even though your symptoms may be the same, you may be suffering from an entirely different illness.
- Keep a list of all drugs you are taking, so your doctor and pharmacist can make appropriate decisions about which medications would be safe.

7. Pass around the different drug labels and have students read the instructions out loud. Assist students who have difficulty reading. Ask the students questions to test their understanding of the instructions. Use the following examples as guides for the questioning.
   - The instructions indicated that a person should take no more than eight pills in a 24-hour period (two every six hours). Is it OK to take three pills every five hours?
   - The instructions indicated that the medication should not be mixed with alcohol. Is it OK to

take the medication and have two beers at dinner?

- The instructions indicated that a person should not operate heavy machinery when taking the medication. Is it OK to drive?
- The instructions indicated that the pills should be taken with food. Is it OK to take the medication and then eat something an hour later?
- The instructions indicated to take the medication until all the pills are gone. Is it OK to stop a few days earlier if you are feeling better?

USING SICK TIME BENEFITS

Objective

1. Identify decisions that need to be made when you are sick and need to go to work.

Instructional Format: This lesson will provide students with the opportunity to practise going through the process of deciding whether to call in sick for work. Start the lesson by simply providing the students with the following scenario: "It is 6 a.m. and you have just waken up and do not feel well. You have to be to work by 7:30 a.m.. What decisions do you need to make?" Allow the students to discuss and think through the process as independently as possible. Guidelines are listed below to provide assistance.

1. How sick are you? If you can answer 'yes' to any of the following questions, it might be a good idea to call in sick.
    - Do you need to see a doctor in order to get better?
    - Do you have an illness (flu, pink eye, etc.) that is contagious?
    - If you go to work, is there a chance that you may get even sicker to the point that you may have to miss more than one day of work?

- If you went to work, would you be unproductive due to the illness?

2. If you decide that it would probably be a good idea to call in sick, consider the following:
   - How much sick time do you have? If you have more than a few days, it might be a good idea to stay home this day to try to get better. If you only have a few days, you may have to decide whether you may need those days at a later date. A person would have to make this decision based on her health history. *For example*, a person may have terrible allergies at the same time every year. That time is coming up and the allergies are worse than how she feels right now.
   - If you do not have sick benefits, can you afford to miss a day's pay?
3. After making the decision to stay at home from work, then you have to do the following:
   - Figure out whether you have any work that someone will have to do for you.
     1. Follow your employer's procedure for calling in sick.
     2. When you speak to your supervisor or the person to whom you call in sick, tell him that you are not feeling well and need to take the day off. Inform the person about responsibilities that will need to get accomplished by another co-worker.
4. For students that may need the practise, do some role-playing of calling in sick. Trainers should model what to say on the phone. When the student is practising, the trainer can play the role of the supervisor.
5. Remind students about the following things in relation to sick time.

- Although sick time is a benefit, it should be used only when necessary. Employers look favourably on employees who do not miss any work due to illness. In fact, some employers give out awards and other incentives to employees who do not use any sick time during a specified period such as an year.
- Employees should stay knowledgeable about how much sick time they have. If their supervisor does not keep them informed, employees should check every month to find out how much sick time they have.
- Employees should know the procedure for calling in sick. Details such as how much notice do you need to give and with whom do you speak are important factors. You may suggest that students put this procedure down in writing and have it close to the phone.
- Many employers prefer that the employee call in sick. If possible, do not ask a family member or friend to call your boss to let her know you are sick.

❑

5

CRISIS MANAGEMENT

OBJECTIVE

1. Use assertive statements to express oneself in various role-plays.

Instructional Format: This topic will mainly involve modelling and role-playing. Trainers will need to do some instruction prior to modelling the assertive behaviours. Trainers will need to take into account the students' verbal abilities when instructing them on assertive messages. It is important that the students become comfortable in using different types of assertive skills. This unit may need to be broken up into multiple sessions in order to practise the skills thoroughly. It is helpful to video-tape role-plays. If you have the equipment, it is highly recommended.

1. Instruct on the "Tips for Being Assertive." Depending on the audience, a trainer may need to limit the information provided in this handout. The suggested components are marked with an asterisk. The role-modelling should then focus on these areas.
2. Instruct on the three different categories of assertive behaviour. Again, depending on the student's comprehension abilities, this information should be modified as needed. According to Cooley and Hollandsworth (1977) and Christoff and Kelly (1985) there are three basic categories of assertive behaviour.

Use the categories listed below as guides for the content of the different assertive messages. Each student should practise the three different types of assertive behaviour.

- *Refusal Assertiveness:* How to say no at the right time and in the right way
- *State your position:* "No, I can't."
- *Explain your reason:* "I have something else to do that day."
- *Express understanding:* "I hope you can find something else."

These skills should be practised in the context of a person trying to get the student to do something that is harmful (use drugs, steal, skip work, etc.) or a person trying to get the student to do something when he she has another commitment (work overtime, babysit, work on a day off). Remind students that they have a right to say no whenever they want, but there may be serious consequences (*i.e.,* boss asks you to do a job, police ask you to pull over, etc.).

The point of saying no is to keep from being taken advantage of or doing something harmful, not to keep from engaging in daily responsibilities. When practicing refusals of harmful behaviour, it is not appropriate to make understanding statements (*i.e.,* I hope you have luck getting someone else to snort cocaine). It is most important to focus on the refusal and the reason.

- *Expressing Feelings:* Telling people how you feel.
- *Express Positive Feelings:* "You did a great job."
- *Express Negative Feelings:* "I am upset by what you did."

There is a unit on expressing negative feelings in the "Anger Management" lesson. In both situations it is helpful to teach the person to give reasons for her feelings, especially when assertively expressing negative feelings. Expressing positive feelings and giving compliments are important skills in building healthy relationships. Complimenting people at work is an excellent way to demonstrate good social skills on the job. It is important for people to distinguish what is appropriate in different situations. *For example*, it is not appropriate for people at work to make statements such as "Good job on that project, I love you!"

- *Request Assertiveness:* To get information, clarification and ask for what you want.
- *State the Problem:* "Boss, you have given two different instructions."
- *Make a Request:* "Can you let me finish one project before starting the other?"
- *Getting Clarification:* "Can you explain what you want done again?"

  Making requests is an important skill, especially on the job site. Remind students that just because they are being assertive, they do not have the right to make any request they want. It is important for students to practise approaching supervisors with different requests. Some examples include getting clarification on an instruction, asking them to do something different when criticising work (*i.e.,* "please do not yell at me in front of co-workers"), asking for time off, asking for different work, etc. Often times, another form of assertiveness is combined with requests. One example is, "I am upset, please do not yell at me in front of the other workers."

3. Model good assertive skills for each of the three categories of assertive behaviour. Do it incorrectly every once in a while to see if the students can correct it.
4. Students should role-play multiple scenarios for each of the three categories of assertive behaviour. There

are some suggested scenarios to role-play under each category of assertive behaviour.

ANGER MANAGEMENT

Anger that leads to physical violence is serious and needs appropriate intervention. An individual who exhibits behaviours that can lead to harm of another or property damage needs psychological services from a professional trained in anger management. This lesson can be used for those individuals whose anger management issues cause them problems (*i.e.*, loss of a job) but do not cause significant harm to themselves or those around them.

Objectives

1. Identify at least three feelings or emotions.
2. Identify the difference between negative ("bad") emotions and negative behaviour.

Instructional Format: This topic will be discussion-based in which the student will learn about feelings and behaviours. The important point to stress is that all feelings are OK, but negative behaviours as a result of those feelings are not.

1. Identify different types of feelings or emotions. Make a list of as many emotions as possible. Use pictures if students need a visual representation of feelings. Leader and participants can also act out different emotions.
2. Identify different situations in which people feel common emotions such as happiness, sadness, anger, fear and excitement. Have the participants describe how they behave in those situations.
3. Differentiate between the feelings of anger and the behaviours of anger. Ask if there are any "bad" emotions. Stress throughout the lesson that anger, sadness, etc., are not bad. "It is OK to be angry, but it is not OK to hit, call people names or yell at people."

Spend time discussing and using examples that differentiate bad behaviour from "bad" emotions. Have participants provide examples from their own lives.

RECOGNISING ANGER

Objectives

1. Identify at least three physiological responses that are cues that a person may be upset.
2. Complete a daily "Anger Journal" for one week.

Instructional Format: This topic will be discussion-based with demonstration of how to do an "Anger Journal." It is important for the participants to understand that how we feel on the inside and what we are showing on the outside gives us clues that we may be angry. If a person can recognise the anger prior to doing something inappropriate, he or she can do something appropriate.

1. Identify how people's bodies feel when they get upset. Use a common example of getting a headache when a person gets angry to help the discussion along. Other common physiological responses include: stomachache, rapid heart rate, perspiring, hot feeling in the neck/face and shaking/trembling.
2. Instruct on how to recognise the signs of getting angry by paying attention to behaviour (raising voice, pacing, rubbing head, etc.) and feelings. Indicate that a person has a choice at this point. He can yell, hit, curse or do something mean or he can do something more appropriate. Appropriate responses to anger will be discussed in future topics.
3. Teach how to use the "Anger Journals." Use the journal that best fits each student's cognitive ability. Anger journals should be done daily. Make sure enough journals are copied for the students to complete multiple weeks of recording. Provide the

students with a rationale for using the logs: (1) it provides information on what upsets a person, (2) it provides information about how they respond, and (3) it can provide information for group discussion.

4. At the end of the first week, the trainer should review the journals with the students. Remember that it is often difficult for people to admit that they have been angry. Thus, it is important to reinforce any attempt to document an episode of anger, regardless of the outcome. Trainers should provide feedback. Students should continue keeping the journals until they have correctly completed one week of recording. However, once the student has mastered the skill of keeping a journal, it would not hurt him to continue keeping a record. Trainers should continue to meet with students on a weekly basis to review the journals.

COPING SKILLS–RELAXATION

Objectives

1. Make a list of at least five activities that they can do that will help them relax.
2. Demonstrate deep-breathing techniques.

Instructional Format: This topic will be discussion-based with rehearsal of the breathing exercises. Focus the discussion on the importance of learning how to calm down prior to responding to a provoking situation. If a person is not calm when confronting a person who has done something to upset her, the chances that she will be successful in using her coping skills are decreased.

1. Discuss that one appropriate response to anger is for the person to relax. List examples of different ways people relax. Each student should make a list of at least five activities that could be used to help her relax. For those students who don't read, have them make a picture list using the supplies listed above.

2. Instruct the students on deep-breathing techniques. Use the information sheet to provide the students with information and instructions. Inform them that they may have to do the deep breathing on the spot without the luxury of a quiet room. Tell them that if they practise, it will be easier to do.
3. Talk to the students about how to appropriately excuse themselves when they need to do deep breathing techniques. They cannot just walk away from their boss when he is yelling at them. Teach the students to use a phrase such as "excuse me, I have to go to the bathroom." At this point the students should practise leaving the area and going to do deep breathing in another area. Again, this will take practise.
4. Summarise the topic. Remind the students that when people get upset, so do their bodies. In order to help them deal with their emotions, they need to keep the feelings in their bodies calm.

COPING SKILLS–SELF-TALK

Objective

1. Complete the steps to self-instruction training during role-plays.

Instructional Format: This topic will use all four of the common teaching methods: Instruction, modelling, role-play and feedback. Trainers will need to teach about how our thoughts can influence our feelings and behaviour. *For example,* if someone bumps into us and we tell ourselves that he did this on purpose, we are more likely to get upset. However, if we tell ourselves that it was an accident, we are less likely to get upset. If we give ourselves good instructions during the provoking situation, we will be more likely to respond appropriately. It is helpful to video-tape role-plays. If you have the equipment, it is highly recommended.

1. Discuss with students the rationale for the topic. Provide information about how our thoughts can influence our emotions. Just as other people can make us feel angry by what they say, we can get ourselves upset by what we say to ourselves. Provide the following examples:
   - Our boss yells at us. If we think that he is out to get us, we will get angry. If we think that he is just having a bad day, we may not get angry or at least as angry.
   - Our co-worker spills something on some copies we just made. If we think she is out to get us fired or into trouble, we will get angry. If we tell ourselves it was just an accident, we are less likely to get angry.
   - Our spouse comes home late. If we think he/she is cheating on us, we are going to get angry. Or, if we think he/she has been in an accident, we may feel worried. If we think he/she is just running late and we will ask him/her were she has been, we are less likely to feel bad.
   - Our child is acting up in the store. If we think he is doing it on purpose and all of the people in the store are angry with us, we may get upset. If we think that there is something wrong with the child and most people probably don't care, we are less likely to get upset.
   - A co-worker brings us a card for our birthday. If we think he really likes us and wants to go out with us, we may have feelings of attraction and a desire to date. If we think that he is just being kind, we will have feelings of friendship, but may not have romantic feelings. (It works for positive feelings too.)
2. Pick a role-play from the role-play scenarios for "Anger Management." Pick a volunteer to role-play

the scenario. The instructor will play the person who is trying to keep from getting angry first. The role-play has examples of appropriate coping statements to use. Read through the "Steps for Anger Control" for further information. The instructor should make the self statements out loud. Depending on the cognitive level of the students, the instructor will have to modify the complexity of the statements.

3. Pick another role-play and have a student practise the coping skills to control anger. The student should do deep breathing while the instructor says the self-statements for the student.
4. Using the same role-play, have the student practise deep breathing while he/she makes the statements out loud.
5. Using the same role-play, have the student practise deep breathing while he/she whispers the statements.
6. Using the same role-play, have the student practise deep breathing while he/she thinks the statements.

CONFLICT RESOLUTION

Objectives

1. Identify different conflicts a person has experienced.
2. Identify appropriate ways to resolve a conflict.
3. Practise the steps to resolve a conflict.

Instructional Format: This topic will involve discussion and practise of conflict resolution skills. The students should have training and/or the skills in communication, assertiveness and anger management. These skills are essential to resolving conflict. Conflict resolution is a difficult skill to master. It is important to stress to the students the importance of using "outs" when their skills are not helping resolve the situation. The "outs" include leaving the area, agreeing to disagree and getting a third party involved to assist in the resolution.

1. Discuss with students different conflicts they have been in. Have them talk about how they resolved it. Discuss the positives and negatives about how they resolved the conflict. Positive ways can include trying to understand the other person's point of view, compromising, talking about it, etc. Negative ways include yelling, refusing to change or compromise, refusing to work out the conflict, etc.
2. Instruct the steps to resolve the conflict. The steps are outlined on the handout titled "Steps to Resolve a Conflict."
3. Role-play situations that allow the students to practise conflict resolution skills. Use situations that the students have brought up in discussion.

STEPS TO RESOLVE

1. *Control Emotions:* Use relaxation techniques. Take yourself out of the situation. Express your feelings assertively.
2. *Identify the Reason for the Conflict:* Who is responsible? If it is needed, take time away from the person to think about the conflict and plan a strategy to resolve.
3. Ask the person if he/she has time to talk.
4. Tell the person how you are feeling (*i.e.,* I am feeling upset right now).
5. Tell the person why you are feeling like you are (*i.e.,* you have not paid your share of the rent for the last two months).
6. Listen. Listen. Listen. Allow the person to respond.
7. Discuss with the person different alternatives for resolving the conflict.
8. Continue to discuss calmly.
9. If the conflict can not be resolved and/or you are getting angry, inform the person that you need to leave and you would like to talk about it later.

GETTING ALONG WITH CO-WORKERS

Objectives

1. Complete "Who I Like to Work With" handout.
2. Explain what to do when you do not get along with somebody.
3. Identify appropriate behaviours and topics of discussion in the workplace.

Instructional Format: This topic will be discussion based. Much of the skills needed to get alongwith co-workers are covered in other lessons such as anger management, conflict resolution, communication skills and employer expectations. If a person can master these other skills, she should be able to get alongwith most people.

This lesson works more on a person's attitude about the people with whom he works. A person does not have a choice about the people he works with, so they have to be understanding of the differences in other people. They may not like everyone they work with, but they have to be able to work with all types of people.

1. Discuss how we will not get along with everyone we work with. Sometimes we don't like how they behave, sometimes we don't like what they believe in and sometimes we don't like how they look. Have the students fill out the handout titled "Who I Like to Work With." Inform the students that the handout is just for them and they will not have to share the information with anyone.
2. Review the terms "prejudice" and "tolerance" with the students. This will help set-up the discussion about how to separate disliking someone because of what she does and disliking someone because she belongs to a certain group.
   - *Prejudice:* According to Webster's Dictionary, prejudice is a preconceived idea; an opinion held in disregard of the facts that contradict it; and/

or, intolerance or hatred. A person is prejudiced toward another person when he does not like or has untrue beliefs about that person because he/ she is part of a certain group. The groups that are usually the focus of prejudice are women, minority races, different religions and homosexuals. However, people can hold prejudices against any person of any group. All lawyers are..., all people from the South are..., people who work in fast food are... The person makes this judgment about the other person without getting to know what that person is like. The judgment may be true, but it has nothing to do with the group he/she belongs to; rather, it has to do with what that person is like. Some examples of prejudices are: Men are only interested in sex, women are weak, Jewish people are stingy, African-Americans are lazy and Asians are smart. It is true that some men are only interested in sex, some women are weak, some Jews are stingy, some blacks are lazy and some Asians are incredibly intelligent. But, you can find these characteristics across all different groups of people. So, when a person is lazy, it is not because of her race; it is because the person is lazy.

The following is another illustration. A co-worker, who is black, takes two days off because her son is sick. The days are during the busiest part of the year for that company and a co-worker automatically assumes she is lazy and says, "Isn't that typical of one of them." This assumption is wrong in two areas. *First*, there are no facts to indicate that African-Americans are a lazy race. There are some blacks who are lazy, but there are also whites who are lazy. Laziness has nothing to do with race; it has to do with the individual person. The second problem is that the person has neglected to notice that this co-worker is one of the hardest working people on the job and the fact is, her child has had a temperature of 104 during these past two days.

- *Tolerance:* According to Webster's Dictionary, tolerance is respecting the beliefs and practises of another person. Thus, when a person does something a different way or holds certain beliefs, you do not condemn that person or interfere with that person. That does not mean you have to agree with that person, it means that you tolerate the way he does things. On the job, there are going to be people who behave in a way that you do not agree with. If that behaviour is interfering with your job or the company, you have the right to talk to that person or go to the supervisor. *For example*, a co-worker may believe it is OK to drink on the job. You do not have to tolerate this. Talk to her or your supervisor. On the other hand, if you did not believe that using drugs or alcohol was OK at any time, you may have a hard time tolerating when someone talks about the parties she goes to on the weekends. If this is the case, you could ask that person not to tell you about his parting on the weekends. But, most likely you will need to tolerate the fact that he drinks outside of work.
- In summary, when we hold prejudices about certain people and are intolerant of their beliefs and practises (when they do not harm anyone), it makes it very difficult to get alongwith others. It is important to get to know the person for who they are and respect that person's beliefs. We are not going to agree with everything a person thinks, says or does, so working with people who are exactly like you is going to be difficult. Remind

students that there are probably people who they are close to that have different beliefs from them. Most people have arguments with family members and friends over what they do and what they believe in, but we do not dislike those people because they are similar to us. Therefore, we should not dislike people who are different from us in skin colour, religion, ethnicity, etc., just because they have different beliefs or practises.

3. Discuss with people why they would not like working with certain people and try to get them to look at why. See if people can recognise the differences between not liking a co-worker because of how they behave (*i.e.,* doing things that cause problems on the job) and not liking a co-worker because of who they are.

   This would be a good time to discuss the exercise on identifying who the student would like to work with. Remember that the information is intended for the student's own use, but allow students to share information if they are willing. Pick out a few of the different "types" of workers and ask the students the following types of questions:

   - "Is this a good reason to not like a person? Why or why not?"
   - "Is that acceptable behaviour at work? Why or why not?"
   - "Did any of your answers change after our discussion?"

4. Make a list of alternatives of what a person can do when they don't get alongwith somebody they work with. If it is because a co-worker is behaving in a certain way that is bothersome or interferes with the job, the person can talk to this person or speak with the boss. Role-play speaking to that person or speaking to a supervisor.

5. If the person just does not like the co-worker, instruct the person to find the positive aspects in the person and try to focus on the good points of the person when working with him/her. Have the students identify a person with whom he/she has not got along and list both the positives and negatives of that person. Discuss.
6. Discuss students' behaviours that make it difficult for co-workers to get along with them. Have the students try to identify areas on which they need to work.
7. Summarise the lesson by listing behaviours that make it difficult for people to get along at work.
   - Talk a lot about their religious or political beliefs
   - Have a poor attitude or an unhappy disposition
   - Unwilling to help
   - Poor work
   - Absent or late a lot
   - Gossip
   - Talk too much
   - Unfriendly
   - Disrespectful to supervisor or co-workers
   - Tell supervisor about things people do wrong all of the time

LEISURE SKILLS

Objectives

1. Identify the benefits of having meaningful activities outside of work.
2. Use a newspaper to identify at least three activities in which you would like to participate.

Instructional Format: This lesson is designed to provide training in the area of leisure skills. Although leisure skills may not appear to be a significant life skill for vocational success, it is important to stress to students that it truly is an important skill. Without meaningful activities to structure a person's time outside of work, there are a number of problems that can occur in relation to work. Part of the lesson will be spent discussing these problems. The rest of the lesson will be spent training students to understand factors that go into selecting leisure activities. There are many skills that are needed to effectively participate in leisure activities. A person needs telephone skills to call and find out about the activity, social skills to interact and make friends with the people at the activity and money management skills to budget the money to participate in the activity. Training in these skills is available in units contained in this manual.

1. Discuss the problems that can occur at work if a person does not use time away from work productively.
   - A person may be more apt to work a lot of overtime. This can lead to feelings of being overworked which can affect job performance.
   - A person may linger around work even when he is not working. People who do this generally do not have a lot of social contacts outside of work. Although this may be enjoyable for the person, his co-workers may be distracted and even annoyed, which does not contribute to a good working environment.
   - A person may be unhappy because of her poor social life. This unhappiness could spill over into the workplace.
   - A person may be involved in destructive activities such as using drugs or alcohol.
   - A final problem can occur when a person uses his free time too productively. When a person gets so involved in activities outside of work that he is not getting enough sleep, is missing work

or is spending money that is needed for essentials, this can interfere with work.

2. Discuss the factors of time, money, people and available activities when developing a meaningful social life.
   - *Time:* Have students make a list of when they generally have free time. This is an important first step in deciding what type of activities a person might pursue. If they want to be involved with a club that only meets on the weekends, but they work on the weekends, it would not be a good idea to actively pursue becoming a member. Stress to students that, although it is good to be involved in activities away from work, they do not want to be involved in so many activities that they are too tired to work.
   - *Money:* Many leisure activities cost money. If an activity costs so much money that a student is having a difficult time paying for rent, groceries, transportation, etc., she may have to change her leisure choices. There are many activities that cost little or no money.
   - *People:* One of the best ways to get involved in leisure activities is to meet people. Of course, a person may have to get involved in an activity first in order to meet people who have the same interests. Remind students that they can meet people in their neighbourhood, church and at work.
   - *Available Activities:* Depending on where a person lives, the number of activities that are available is going to vary. A person living in a larger city is going to have a greater selection of activities than person living in a small town. Remind students that most towns have holy places, parks and opportunities to volunteer.

3. Pass out the newspapers to the students and have them look through the sections that contain listings of activities going on in the community. Remind students about movies and other entertainment, sports, outdoor recreation, volunteer opportunities and clubs. Have them identify three activities they would like to participate in over the next few weeks. Remind them to consider cost, time available and transportation. Have students discuss why they would be interested in participating in the activities they chose.
4. As an optional activity, have the students meet in two weeks without a trainer and have them discuss whether they participated in any of the activities. Have them discuss cost, whether they enjoyed it and whether they met people at the activity that they may do something with in the future.

DECISION MAKING

Objective

1. Identify the steps in a standard process to solve problems and make decisions.

Instructional Format: This lesson is designed for people with average intelligence. A separate lesson contains training on alternative problem-solving techniques for people with mental disabilities. Problem-solving is a cognitive skill that is difficult for many people, regardless of intelligence. After working through the problem-solving process, discuss handling problems in a crisis situation. The process that is presented below is frequently credited to D'Zurilla and Goldfried (1971).

1. Instruct the students on the process to solve a problem or make a decision. It is suggested that the trainer write the steps on the board.
   1. *Define the Problem:* A person can not solve a problem until he clearly understands and

identifies the problem. Try to label the problem in precise and concrete terms. *For example,* "Joe can't drive me to work" identifies a potential problem. However, it may or may not be a problem depending on other factors. The definition above describes the cause of a potential problem. Rephrasing the problem to "How will I get to work?" puts the focus of the problem-solving on getting to work rather than on the fact that Joe stood you up. The fact that Joe can't drive you to work may not be a problem if you have other alternatives. When Joe told you he could not drive affects the significance of the problem. If he told you two days ago, you have less of a problem than if he called 45 minutes before work. A better definition of the problem is "I have to be to work in 45 minutes, my usual ride is not going to show up and the next bus won't get me to work on time."

2. *Develop Alternative Solutions:* This is better known as brainstorming. No idea is a bad one. Each idea could be a possible solution. Try to predict your ability to accomplish each solution and predict the consequences. Using the example above, you may consider calling a taxi. In evaluating this alternative, factors such as cost and whether the taxi can get you to work on time would need to be considered. Have the class generate solutions to solve the problem proposed above.
3. *Make a Decision and Execute:* Pick the best solution and solve the problem using the solution you picked. Have the class pick the best solution to get to work on time.
4. *Evaluate the Outcome:* This is where a lot of learning takes place. If the outcome was successful, then the person learns that this is a good solution if the problem arises again. If it

was unsuccessful, the person knows that it would be best not to try that solution in the future.

2. Pose various problems to the students and have them use the process from above to solve the problem. Use a marker board to write the alternative solutions the class generates. If necessary, the trainer should model this process again for further instruction. The problems below may be defined well enough to complete the first step in the process. However, always clarify and ask "What is the problem?" Let the students work through the process as independently as possible. Once they pick a solution and decide how to execute it, present a likely outcome for them to evaluate.
   - You see your best friend at work take some money that does not belong to him.
   - Your boss asks you to work overtime, but your son needs to be picked up from school.
   - You do not have enough money to pay this month's rent.
   - You are laid off from your job.
   - Your car needs brakes and you do not have enough in savings to pay to fix it.
   - A customer approaches you and complains about the service she received from another worker.
   - You break something at work.
   - Somebody at work borrowed Rs. 887 from you and has not paid you back.
3. *Discuss Solving a Problem in a Crisis:* What is a crisis for some people is not a crisis for others. Ask for examples of what the students consider crises. With the help of the students, discuss why it is difficult to make decisions during a crisis. To begin with, decisions that need to be made tend to be harder to make. This could be why a person is in crisis. They have put off making a tough decision or solving a

problem until it was an emergency situation. One example is not deciding to go to the doctor for minor chest pains until the chest pains are unbearable. Another problem with making decisions in a crisis is people tend to be emotional, making it difficult to think clearly. A third problem with making decisions during a crisis is that they often need to be made in a hurry. This leaves less time to develop possible solutions. Discuss other factors that the students contribute.

4. Review some strategies for crisis management.
    - *Be Prepared:* A person can't be prepared for everything. However, some of these suggestions should help. Develop a savings account to prepare for the possibility of losing a job or making an emergency purchase. Keep some extra money at home for taxi or bus fare. Keep a spare tire, jumper cables and other emergency equipment in your car. Keep your home safe with fire alarms, locks on cabinets where poisons and medications are and a phone list with emergency numbers.
    - If a crisis does develop, try to stay as calm as possible. Keeping a cool head will increase the likelihood that you will make good decisions.
    - Take as much time as possible to make a decision. Even if you are under a time crunch, it may be better to make the right decision a little late than a wrong decision early.
    - Get assistance. Rely on other people to help you through the crisis.

PROBLEM-SOLVING PROCEDURES

Objective

1. Identify the steps in a modified process to solve problems and make decisions.

Instructional Format: This lesson will provide additional problem-solving procedures for those students who may find the standard process too complex. Researchers have been successful in training people with developmental disabilities to problem solve (Hughes, Hugo & Blatt, 1996, Hughes & Rusch, 1989, Park and Gaylord, 1989). Students will learn best if they try to solve real-life problems instead of hypothetical problems. There are some "real-life" problems suggested, but they may be difficult to implement. Hypothetical problems also are suggested.

1. The process described below was shown to work with people with severe mental retardation to solve problems (Hughes, 1992). Trainers should utilise self-instruction training (see "Teaching Strategies" at the beginning of the manual) to train students in this process. Use an example of spilling a bucket of water at work to demonstrate this process.
    1. State the problem–"The floor is wet. It is dangerous."
    2. Make a generic response to fix the problem–"I need to clean it up."
    3. Make a specific response to fix the problem–"I need to go to the janitor's closet and get a mop, a bucket and a wet floor sign."
    4. Provide a self-report–"I have mopped up the water."
    5. Provide self-reinforcement–"Good job."
2. Pose the following problems to the students and train them to use this process when solving the problem. Instead of describing the steps as they are listed above, use the following prompts: What is the problem? What do you need to do? How are you going to do it? Did you fix the problem? Did you do a good job?
    - Spill a cup of coffee, can of pop or some other liquid. Have a mop and bucket available.

- During vocational training, assign a task to a student, but do not give him all of the materials to complete the task.
- Bring some type of battery-operated gadget (flashlight, toy, radio) with dead batteries in it. Have a student try to turn it on. Prompt her to try to figure out the problem. Have different types of batteries on hand.
- Bring a television to class. Set it up, but do not plug it in. Tell the class that they are going to watch a short video. When it does not turn on, ask a student for assistance.

3. If these problem situations can not be practiced in the classroom, pose the following hypothetical situations for the students to try to work through.
   - You just missed your bus to take you to work.
   - A coworker tells you to clean the floors, but your boss wants you to empty garbage. You want to be helpful to the coworker.
   - A neighbour keeps trying to borrow money from you. He never pays you back and you never have enough money to buy things you need.
4. Discuss a final strategy for solving problems. This process is actually a series of questions that might be more understandable for people with mental retardation (Foxx and Bittle, 1989).
   - Who should I talk to?
   - Where should I look for help?
   - What should I say?
   - When will the problem be solved?

Have the students answer these questions in an attempt to solve any of the problems in this lesson or the previous one. Have the students actually practise what they will say to the person from whom they are getting help.

❑❑

Other Books on

GENERAL SERIES

1.	Helpline for Stressed Parents **(New)**	175/-
2.	Grow Rich with Peace of Mind **(New)**	175/-
3.	How to be Fit & Young **(New)**	175/-
4.	How to Succeed in Life **(New)**	175/-
5.	100 Ways to Develop Self Confidence **(New)**	160/-
6.	Child Development **(New)**	195/-
7.	Abraham Lincoln A Complete Biography	195/-
8.	Mein Kampf My Struggle	195/-
9.	Think and Grow Rich	150/-
10.	The Art of Personality Development	150/-
11.	Positive Mind Power	160/-
12.	Travel & Tourism An Industry Facilitator	295/-
13.	World's Great Authors And Poets	125/-
14.	Judgment No Aircrash No Death	250/-
15.	Effective Editing Help Yourself in Becoming a Good Editor	150/-
16.	Smart House-Keeping for Modern Women	150/-
17.	Develop Super Power Memory	125/-
18.	World's Great Personalities	150/-
19.	Personality Plus	125/-
20.	Power of Positive Thinking	125/-
21.	Art of Successful Parenting	150/-
22.	A Handbook of Etiquettes	125/-
23.	How to Beat Your Competitors	150/-
24.	How to Negotiate Effectively	150/-
25.	World's Great Scientists	150/-
26.	Patriot: The Unique Indian Leader Netaji Subhas Chandra Bose	250/-
27.	Body Language	125/-
28.	Art of Successful Living	150/-
29.	Make Your Boss Happy	125/-
30.	Jokes for All	125/-
31.	Selected Dohas	295/-

32. Baby Names for Girls **(New)** 125/-
33. Baby Names for Boys **(New)** 125/-
34. Art of Public Speaking 125/-
35. The World's Greatest Speeches 125/-
36. Group Discussions 110/-
37. Personality Development 110/-
38. Think Positive & Things Will Go Right 110/-
39. Once in a Blue Moon (A Tantra Tale) 125/-
40. God is Dead 125/-
41. Travel India (A Complete Guide for Tourists) 295/-
42. Glimpses of Urdu Poetry 450/-
43. Indian Mythology 195/-
44. How to Reduce Tension 125/-
45. A Book of Stenography 150/-
46. Business Letters 125/-
47. Baby Names for the Boy 95/-
48. Baby Names for the Girl 95/-
49. Non Vegetarian Delights 125/-
50. Pure Vegetarian Delights 125/-

Lotus PRESS

Unit No. 220, 2nd Floor, 4735/22, Prakash Deep Building,
Ansari Road, Darya Ganj, New Delhi- 110002
Ph.: 32903912, 23280047, 9811594448
E-mail : lotuspress1984@gmail.com, www.lotuspress.co.in